THE INDEPENDENT
WORLD CUP
CRICKET'87

Martin Johnson & Henry Blofeld
Photography by Michael Steele

❦ THE INDEPENDENT

The Kingswood Press
an imprint of William Heinemann Ltd
10 Upper Grosvenor Street, London W1X 9PA

LONDON MELBOURNE
JOHANNESBURG AUCKLAND

0-434-98142-7 (cloth)
0-434-98146-X (paper)
Produced, edited and designed by First Editions,
27 Palmeira Mansions,
Church Road, Hove,
East Sussex, BN3 2FA.
Typeset by Presentia Art, Horsham.
Printed in Great Britain by Purnell Book Production Limited, Paulton.

Contents

Reports are dated according to publication in *The Independent*.

Introduction

Cricket fans in Britain were on dawn patrol for a month, transistors crackling with news from the sub-continent, as the fourth World Cup unfolded into a series of dramatic and compelling one-day contests which ended with England's narrow loss to Australia in the final.

Seven runs made the difference between success and failure for Mike Gatting's team – but the fact that it was England and Australia who eventually fought it out for the trophy was one of the tournament's many unexpected delights.

There was incident in profusion – notably Javed Miandad's brush with Gatting and the England captain's ill-fated reverse sweep in the final – and a wealth of exciting finishes, from the opening round of matches to the climax in front of 90,000 at the steamy Eden Gardens Stadium.

Many had felt that it had been written in the stars that the co-hosts India and Pakistan would meet in the final but, by batting first and compiling large totals in the semi-finals, the Aussies and the Poms confounded expectation, Allan Border leading his team to their first World Cup.

The details from all the games are to be found on the following pages, as is the expert comment of *The Independent's* Martin Johnson and Henry Blofeld, who saw every significant ball bowled. The pictures of Michael Steele add an extra dimension to the reportage.

We feel it is an authentic document of an exciting and historic tournament.

Charles Burgess, Sports Editor.

World Cup '87 Preview
The Venues

Group A
Australia (captain: Allan Border)
India (captain: Kapil Dev)
New Zealand (captain: Jeff Crowe)
Zimbabwe (captain: John Traicos)

Group B
England (captain: Mike Gatting)
Pakistan (captain: Imran Khan)
Sri Lanka (captain: Duleep Mendis)
West Indies (captain: Viv Richards)

Group A

9 Oct: India v Australia	(Madras)
10 Oct: New Zealand v Zimbabwe	(Hyderabad)
13 Oct: Australia v Zimbabwe	(Madras)
14 Oct: India v New Zealand	(Bangalore)
17 Oct: India v Zimbabwe	(Bombay)
19 Oct: Australia v New Zealand	(Indore)
22 Oct: India v Australia	(New Delhi)
23 Oct: New Zealand v Zimbabwe	(Calcutta)
26 Oct: India v Zimbabwe	(Ahmedabad)
27 Oct: Australia v New Zealand	(Chandigarh)
30 Oct: Australia v Zimbabwe	(Cuttack)
31 Oct: India v New Zealand	(Nagpur)

Group B

8 Oct: Pakistan v Sri Lanka	(Hyderabad)
9 Oct: England v West Indies	(Gujranwala)
12 Oct: Pakistan v England	(Rawalpindi)
13 Oct: Sri Lanka v West Indies	(Karachi)
16 Oct: Pakistan v West Indies	(Lahore)
17 Oct: England v Sri Lanka	(Peshawar)
20 Oct: Pakistan v England	(Karachi)
21 Oct: Sri Lanka v West Indies	(Kanpur)
25 Oct: Pakistan v Sri Lanka	(Faisalabad)
26 Oct: England v West Indies	(Jaipur)
30 Oct: England v Sri Lanka	(Pune)
30 Oct: Pakistan v West Indies	(Karachi)

Semi Finals

4 Nov: Pakistan v Australia	(Lahore)
5 Nov: India v England	(Bombay)

Final

8 Nov Australia v England	(Calcutta)

World Cup '87 Preview
The Teams

AUSTRALIA
Captain: Allan Border

After last winter's dismal showing in their own country, the selectors have discarded one or two familiar names and – as the Australians are never afraid to do – gone for youth.

Tim Zoehrer, Greg Matthews, Merv Hughes and Greg Ritchie have been forsaken, and there are four uncapped players in the squad, the Western Australian batsmen Mike Veletta and Tom Moody, and the South Australian bowlers, Andrew Zesers and Tim May.

Moody is a highly-promising batsman, but none of the others impressed on the England tour, and if May is rated the most promising off-spinner in Australia, they're more badly off for slow bowlers than England. Peter Taylor (a panic/inspired selection for the Sydney Test?) is included, and if he plays will confuse one or two batsmen by tossing it up and attempting to spin it.

Could take 4 for 20, or 1 for 70. Bruce Reid is a class pace bowler, but Craig McDermott was about Pringle's pace the last time England saw him, and the Australians might find themselves chasing one or two daunting totals.

A R Border (capt), **G R Marsh** (vice-capt), **D C Boon, G C Dyer, D M Jones, C J McDermott, T B A May, T M Moody, S P O'Donnell, B A Reid, P L Taylor, M R Veletta, S R Waugh, A K Zesers.**

ENGLAND
Mike Gatting

Handicapped by the absence of Ian Botham and David Gower, but England still have potential match-winning batsmen in Mike Gatting, Chris Broad, and Allan Lamb. The attack is well-balanced, although it will be interesting to see if England play both John Emburey and Eddie Hemmings to the exclusion of a seamer – especially against Pakistan's batsmen, who traditionally tuck into off-spinners with a rare degree of relish.

Paul Downton, who made 1,000 runs for Middlesex this season, adds weight to the batting, which otherwise has a fragile look once past Lamb at No. 5. Emburey, DeFreitas, Pringle and Foster can all bat, but Peter Willey and David Capel would have given it a more solid feel.

So often in one-day matches, saving runs in the field can make the crucial difference, and England seem decidedly unathletic in one or two areas, especially when it's time to vacate the close-catching positions.

DeFreitas, one of the best fielders in the tournament, is likely to be guaranteed a place for that reason alone.

M W Gatting (capt), **J E Emburey** (vice-capt), **C W J Athey, B C Broad, P A J DeFreitas, P R Downton, P W Jarvis, A J Lamb, D R Pringle, R T Robinson, G C Small.**

INDIA
Kapil Dev

India, the holders of the World Cup, are, like Sri Lanka, being reticent about naming their final group of 14 players. The eventual list is likely to be similar to most of their sides over the last few years – and in their own conditions they will never be an easy side to beat.

They must be the favourites to win their group, and in one-day cricket there is no more explosive player in the game today than their captain Kapil Dev.

Probably the single most important player under him will be Ravi Shastri who has made such a reputation as a one-day all-rounder especially in Australia.

This competition will see Sunil Gavaskar's last appearance for his country and he will presumably open with Kris Srikkanth who is the most exciting opening batsman in the game.

The bowling may not be as dangerous as it was in 1984, but Roger Binny remains a most useful all-rounder.

Kapil Dev (capt), **D B Vengsarkhar** (vice-capt), **J Arun Lal, M Azharuddin, K Bhaskar Pillai, R M H Binny, S M Gavaskar, R R Kulkarni, Maninder Singh, S V Manjrekar, K S More, Navjot Singh Sidhu, C S Pandit, M Prabhakar, K Abdul Qayyum, Alay Sharma, Chetan Sharma, Gopal Sharma, Sanjeev K Sharma, R J Shastri, L Shivaramakrishnan, K Srikkanth, S Viswanath, N S Yadav, Rajesh Yadav.**

NEW ZEALAND
Jeff Crowe

New Zealand will have to get the better of either India or Australia if they are to go through to the semi-finals and without Richard Hadlee they are going to find it difficult.

None the less, their new captain, Jeff Crowe, is extremely confident of success, and he may well rejuvenate a side which, although successful in recent years, began to look a little tired under Jeremy Coney against the West Indies earlier this year.

In his brother Martin he has under him arguably the best batsman in the world, but now Bruce Edgar has retired, the batting looks a little vulnerable. Phil Horne may open with John Wright but he, like Ken Rutherford and Dipak Patel, has yet to prove himself at this level.

There is a sameness about much of the bowling. Ewan Chatfield may not be so effective without Hadlee, Martin Snedden and Willie Watson are at best steady while Danny Morrison, who may turn out to be the quickest of the lot, is still untried. They do have two experienced spinners, Stephen Boock and John Bracewell, but will do well to reach the last four.

J J Crowe (capt), **J G Wright** (vice-capt), **S L Boock, J G Bracewell, E J Chatfield, M D Crowe, P A Horne, A N Jones, D K Morrison, D N Patel, K R Rutherford, I D S Smith, M C Snedden, W Watson.**

PAKISTAN
Imran Khan

Beaten by England in the Perth Challenge, again in the Sharjah Trophy, and again in this summer's Texaco series, Pakistan are none the less well fancied to win the World Cup in the sub-continent.

They are a team of rich talent, now with a depth in bowling to match their powerful batting, and, as they are liable to fragment under pressure, Imran Khan's stabilising influence as captain is priceless to them. They beat India 5-1 in last winter's one-day series in India.

Imran, Wasim Akram, Mudassar Nazar, and Imran's tip for the top who flew home injured from England, Saleem Jaffer, represent a quality seam attack, and together with Abdul Qadir, they are capable of defending low totals. Not that their batting line-up suggests they'll have to. They can all bat, and Javed Miandad, who initially threatened to withdraw without a pay rise, is even more dangerous when there are a few extra rupees to be had for stirring deeds.

Imran Kahn (capt), **Javed Miandad** (vice-capt), **Abdul Qadir, Amir Akbar, Asif Mutjaba, Azeem Hafeez, Ijaz Ahmed, Ijaz Faqih, Iqbal Qasim, Mansoor Elahi, Mohsin Kamal, Mudassar Nazar, Ramiz Raja, Sajad Akbar, Saleem Jaffer, Salim Malik, Salim Yousuf, Shaukat Mirza, Shoabib Mohammad, Tauseef Ahmed, Waheed Niazi, Wasim Akram, Zahoor Elahi, Zakir Khan, Zuiqarnain.**

SRI LANKA
Duleep Mendis

Although Sri Lanka's selectors are taking their time to make up their minds over the final squad of 14 players, it will be most surprising if they do not choose many of the players who took part in England in 1984.

They will again be captained by Duleep Mendis, who went so close to scoring two separate hundreds in Sri Lanka's first Test match in England, at Lord's in 1984. His probable vice-captain will be Roy Dias, who is another exciting stroke-maker, and with Kuruppu, Madugalle and Ranatunga to back them up, England and Pakistan will have to watch they do not score an embarrassing number of runs.

Their bowling will be the weakest aspect of their cricket and once again they may decide to rely on those two, old warhorses, de Mel and John. J R Ratnayake is also a useful fast-medium seamer with excellent control, while Ranatunga can also contribute with the seam, but like Zimbabwe they are short of anyone with genuine pace.

L R D Mendis (capt), **S D Anurasiri, R G de Alwis, A F L de Mel, P A de Silva, R L Dias, A P Gurusinha, S Jeganathan, V B John, S M S Kaluperuma, D S B P Kuruppu, A K Kuruppuarachchi, G F Labrooy, R S Madugalle, R S Mahanma, C P Ramanayake, S K Ranasinghe, A Ranatunga, R J Ratnayake, J R Ratnayake, M A R Samarasekera, A Samasekers, S A R Silva, H P Tillekeratne.**

WEST INDIES
Viv Richards

The odds against a Caribbean victory are tempting enough on the face of it but they have not been quite the same unit under Viv Richards as they used to be under Clive Lloyd's captaincy. They are by no means the invincible force they once were, and have also been hit by voluntary absenteeism.

Courtney Walsh, Winston Benjamin, Patrick Patterson, Tony Gray and Eldine Baptiste still represent a high-quality pace attack, but without Malcolm Marshall, Joel Garner, and the now retired Michael Holding, there is a definite hint of inexperience.

The rule prohibiting short-pitched deliveries that pass above a batsman at shoulder height certainly does them no favours, and if they do fail to blast sides out, it will place even more pressure on their batsmen to make big totals, and it was their failure which resulted in not qualifying for either the Perth Challenge or WSC finals in Australia last winter.

Two batting newcomers are 24-year-old Phil Simmons from Trinidad, who replaces Gordon Greenidge, and Carl Hooper of Guyana.

I V A Richards (capt), **R A Harper** (vice-capt), **E A E Baptiste, W K M Benjamin, C A Best, P J L Dujon, A H Gray, D L Haynes, C L Hooper, A L Logie, B P Patterson, R B Richardson, V Simmons, C A Walsh.**

ZIMBABWE
John Traicos

Zimbabwe became a significant cricket factor at Trent Bridge in June 1983 when they beat Australia in the World Cup. They went on to cause more tremors in that competition and have earned the respect of opponents since.

Four years on the team is largely the same as that which performed so creditably in England. The only important absentee is the retired David Fletcher.

Zimbabwe are now captained by probably the last former South African Test cricketer still on the active list. John Traicos is 40 but bowling his off-breaks as well as ever and using his tactical knowledge to get the best out of what is almost entirely an amateur side.

The bowling is much the same as last time with Philip Rawson, Ian Butchart, Kevin Curran and Traicos bearing the brunt.

The batting has the depth if not the talent it might have if Graeme Hick's ambitions had remained with Zimbabwe. The principal run scorers are likely to be Paterson, Pycroft, Houghton, Shah and Curran. In all, Zimbabwe are a good enough side to take full advantage if any of their opponents should falter.

A J Traicos (capt), **D L Houghton** (vice-capt), **K Arnott, E A Brandes, R D Brown, I P Butchart, K M Curran, K G Duers, M A Meman, G A Paterson, A J Pycroft, P W E Rawson, A H Shah, A C Waller.**

Dulux, one of the many sub sponsors of the first World Cricket Cup to take place outside England.

Cricket's fourth World Cup clears the political hurdles to open on two stages, but England face a struggle to bask in the final spotlight.

Assuming there was no last-minute demand for the players to report to immigration, armed with affidavits from their greengrocers to the effect that they've not been near a Cape apple, England will have booked into their Delhi hotel this morning to confirm their participation in cricket's fourth World Cup.

It is the first time the event will have been held outside this country and, after months of attempted political interference, the host nations ultimately deemed the competition too important to sacrifice on the altar of South Africa. What we have here is the equivalent of a game of football on Christmas Day, after which it's back to the trenches.

The final is scheduled for Calcutta on 8 November, although as nothing ever quite runs to plan on the sub-continent ("no problem" is the standard euphemism for "I know all the kit has been sent to Jaipur, the match is in Bombay, and you're stuck in Pune, but don't worry . . ."), it's best not to regard it as concrete. Whenever, wherever, it's a shade of odds-against England being involved.

This might appear unduly pessimistic in the light of four consecutive one-day international tournament victories . However, the fact that it might be a touch harder to pick up the sound of popping champagne corks through the nation's transistors this winter than it was last, has less to do with the licensing laws than the absence of dissenting personnel.

England can get round the former by the routine expedient of registering as alcoholics, but, thanks largely to the numbing amount of international cricket, it might be more a case of alcoholics anonymous – and that goes for the West Indies and New Zealand, too.

David Gower, Ian Botham, Richard Hadlee, Malcolm Marshall, Joel Garner and Gordon Greenidge are all notable absentees, and while it may not be unconnected with the prospect of six weeks on the sub-continent (Botham regards it as somewhere to send the mother-in-law and Gower prefers a winter on the piste), modern demands on top players have turned even a prestigious tournament such as this into just another routine day at the office.

Last winter's tour to Australia was arduous enough, but by comparison it was a mere jog around the block.

For nine of the players, after the following three-Test series in Pakistan, there's just enough time to nip back and pull a couple of Christmas crackers before it's off again to New Zealand and Australia. Then the computer appears to have slipped up badly. Unless it can cough up a Test to commemorate something meaningful (the 10th anniversary of the

Trent Bridge pavilion tea urn perhaps), it's 10 days off until pre-season training.

Peter Lush, who was last week given a three-year appointment as England overseas tour manager, conceded that this winter would be "appreciably tougher" than last, although as he well knows from experience in Australia, winning is a potent antidote against the weekly grind of play-travel-practice.

As far as the pre-Christmas leg goes, winning the World Cup might prove to be a more feasible objective than the following series in Pakistan, where even now groundsmen will be preparing their pitches armed with a bucket of plasticine, and where umpires will look more sympathetically than ours upon appeals for one-handed catches on the bounce, as practised in school playgrounds and by Salim Yousuf, and championed by Hasib Ahsan.

If England are to qualify from their group, it may have to be at the expense of the weakened West Indies rather than Pakistan, who are favourites to win the event for the first time. There is, though, leaving aside the unavoidable absences of Gower and Botham, the nagging feeling that the selectors did not quite make the best of the talent available to them.

This applies both to the World Cup, for which Peter Willey, David Capel and Ashley Metcalfe were all obvious candidates, and also for the Test series.

In that particular case, this summer's form appears to have counted for substantially less than having been part of the triple crown-winning squad in Australia.

Historic evidence suggests that dinosaurs never ventured further north of what is now Scratchwood Services, in which case Peter May has even more in common with that creature than we thought.

Asked why Jonathan Agnew (101 wickets) had not been included, May replied that he was worried about his fitness. Agnew sent down more overs in the County Championship last season than any other pace bowler – 512 more than Graham Dilley managed, and 427 more than Gladstone Small achieved. This does not exactly suggest diligent research on the part of the England chairman.

There is more hope, though, to be gleaned from Mike Gatting's leadership, and if he can rekindle last winter's remarkable team spirit, then those planning to be up with the milkman for live coverage again this winter, may yet find some kind of antidote to the weather.

Gatting's rude awakening

Mike Gatting will have to get himself a more powerful alarm clock than the one that failed to wake him in Melbourne last winter. England's opening match in the World Cup will give a whole new meaning to the term pyjama cricket – a four o'clock get-out-of-bed call, a 6 am coach ride from Lahore to Gujranwala, and a 9 am start against the West Indies.

Daylight disappears like a power cut in the sub-continent, and early kick-offs are essential to get through 50 overs per side in a day. Rapidly

Gatting flexing his muscles with the aid of Laurie Brown.

fading light decrees that the cut-off time for a finish is 5 pm, which could lead to some games being decided on run-rate, and slow over-rates will be dealt with by swingeing fines.

Teams failing to complete 50 overs within the allotted $3\frac{1}{2}$ hours will have to cough up £1,000 for finishing one short, plus an additional £1,400 for each extra one. Those sums will be doubled for the semi-finals and final, and with only £30,000 on offer for the whole tournament, someone could end up in the red.

This places a heavy premium on bowlers' accuracy, and wides could prove expensive in more ways than one. As in Australia last winter, the square-leg umpire will call anything bouncing above the batsman's shoulders.

Foster sees if his helmet still fits.

England stay serene in sea of chaos

England's cricketers, complete with doctor, diet sheets and microwave oven, arrived in New Delhi yesterday and immediately looked distinctly out of place.

If they are well prepared for the sub-continent's first World Cup, no one else appears to be. By virtue of being the last of the eight competing teams to get here, England have a fair amount of catching up to do in the early chaos stakes.

The West Indies took an early lead by failing to get visas for entry to Pakistan, thus adding to what is in any case a near-terminal blockage of red tape, but they were quickly overhauled by both India and Pakistan, who have an established pedigree in such matters.

Pakistan have announced, unilaterally it appears, that whether they qualify first or second from Group B (which also involves England, West Indies and Sri Lanka), they intend to play their semi-final, come what may, on home ground in Lahore.

India, already guaranteed the final in Calcutta on 8 November, appear to have gone along with this, probably because they were having too many problems of their own last night to care. So should England go through with Pakistan their semi-final would now appear to be booked for Bombay.

Less than six hours before the midnight deadline, India had still not announced their squad of 14 to the World Cup organising committee, because of a row between their board and some senior players – notably the captain Kapil Dev and Sunil Gavaskar – over the wearing of official logos.

Not long ago Kapil and Gavaskar were fined by their board for contravening ICC regulations and wearing "oversize" logos promoting their individual sponsors, an insurance company called Reliance. Now the board are telling them to wear the same logos for nothing – the company being the official World Cup sponsors – and Kapil and Gavaskar, for two, do not think much of it.

The odds were still in favour of their signing contracts inside the deadline, but it has further angered officials, who regard it as more evidence of a "make-a-fast-rupee" mentality among their leading players. They have already given way to demands to up the match fees from 3,500 rupees (£140) to 5,000 rupees (£200), and offer other incentives of R500 per boundary and R1,000 per wicket.

That does not sound a lot, but Indian cricket is not exactly rolling around in a bottomless well of rupees, and, in this part of the world, wealthy, cricket-mad businessmen are so thick on the ground that a board official is quite likely to find himself knocked off his bicycle by a freebie Cadillac driven by one of the "stars".

The police also have their problems trying to halt a flood of forged tickets for today's inaugural ceremony and friendly match in Delhi (if there is ever such a thing between India and Pakistan) after discovering an unofficial printing press at one of the group's venues, Indore.

All this made the problems of Dicky Bird, who along with David Shepherd is representing England on the umpiring panel, seem pretty small beer. Bird, 2-1 on to suffer the first English calamity of the trip, lost a tooth chewing on a bar of toffee. His own fault, really, he conceded. Geoff Boycott told him to eat nothing but bars of fruit and nut.

England, acting on rather more highly-qualified dietary advice, spent yesterday relaxing after their flight and taking meals out of the microwave. With outside temperatures hovering around 100F, they could just as well have fried an egg on the pavement, but the doctor has advised against it.

DATELINE DELHI, 1 /10 /87, MARTIN JOHNSON REPORTS . . .

Crease peace breaks out

It is doubtful whether it could happen anywhere else. India and Pakistan, whose armed forces spent the previous night shooting each other, unofficially fought the fourth World Cup in Delhi yesterday in a 45-over friendly and sporting the official tournament logo "Cricket for Peace".

Cricket being slightly more important than war in this part of the world (the morning paper headline "Cup Fever Mounts" dwarfed "150 Pak Troops Killed In Clashes"), the day began with the Indian Cricket Board giving in to a string of last-minute demands from their leading players rather than run the risk of having to field a weakened team.

Kapil Dev and Sunil Gavaskar were among 10 players who refused to sign their World Cup contracts unless several restrictive clauses were removed – among them the right to wear individual as well as official logos. Cricket for peace is all very well, but cricket for cash won this time.

It all seemed a bit nonsensical, anyway, with the umpires walking out wearing jackets with the name of a whiskey firm emblazoned across the back, and this does not look destined to be remembered as a "ran like clockwork" World Cup. Ran like one of the Delhi taxis more likely, which have an engine note not dissimilar to the African Queen, and appear to be licensed exclusively for retired *kamikaze* pilots.

It is difficult to believe that India, where everybody is too busy being helpful and charming to step on a few toes and get things done, will be anything other than pleasantly chaotic. If their competition chairman N K P Salve is to be believed, he bid for the World Cup only out of pique at being refused four complimentary tickets for pals for the '83 final at Lord's.

One thing the Indians have got sewn up, however, is security. Talking of Lord's, you will be startled to know that they are not in the same league on the Grace Gates, where the wrong-coloured tickets might get you a "sorry, more than the job's worth", but the MCC do appear to draw the line at sub-machine guns. The Prime Minister Rajiv Gandhi was late for the opening ceremony yesterday, probably because he was being frisked at the turnstile.

He did not stay for much of the match either – possibly because he was thirsty or had a 'phone call to make. With a fair cross-section of the world's cricketing press in the Nehru Stadium, there was neither a telephone nor telex in sight, and with temperatures up in the high nineties, the organisers had decreed that the only thing necessary to human life was salted potato crisps.

Whether the absence of liquid inside had anything to do with the fact that the game was organised in aid of the Indian drought relief fund, the worthy cause made it nice to see the stadium to about two-thirds of its 75,000 capacity.

Normally, there is no need for the equivalent of Michael Fish in India, because he would have to come on only twice a year. In June "it's going to rain for four months" and in October "it's not going to rain for eight months". This time, though, even the world's wettest place (Cherapunjee in the Himalayan foothills), only 500km or so from Delhi, has had the occasional spot of play before lunch.

Yesterday, they were playing after supper – a coloured-clothing day-night match under giant Meccano-like floodlights. The first ever day-nighter here was abandoned when they fused, but they lasted the course this time, and India won by 14 runs. One suspects that Pakistan will represent more formidable opposition in the competition proper.

The game was prefaced by a ceremonial letting off of balloons (most of which remained grounded and held up the start) and with all eight nations being introduced to the PM. England's vice-captain, John Emburey, missed the presentation after spraining an ankle the previous evening playing tennis with Graham Gooch. Happily, it is not serious. Today England fly to Pakistan to prepare for their opening group match against the West Indies tomorrow week.

DATELINE ISLAMABAD, 2 /10 /87, MARTIN JOHNSON REPORTS . . .

England hit by middle disorder

A mild outbreak of what is known at home, if not among the locals, as Delhi belly, disrupted England's first tour practice session at the city's National Stadium yesterday.

First news of the casualties came from manager Micky Stewart with the words: "Gatt's got a bit of a gut," which taken one way was not exactly exclusive information, although the England captain turned out to be the worst affected of half a dozen players.

He was not well enough to make it to the ground but Graham Gooch, Derek Pringle, Paul Jarvis and Bill Athey all took some part in between various emergency excursions indoors.

Two other players also gave the session a miss. John Emburey remained at the team hotel with his sprained ankle and Phillip DeFreitas sat under a shady tree watching the others sweat, albeit not feeling well enough to count himself fortunate. DeFreitas apparently arrived under the weather, and Stewart thinks it may be a reaction to an innoculation.

Everyone else seemed in good nick, apart possibly from Allan Lamb, who may have a touch of *absent frienditis*. Without Ian Botham and David Gower, Lamb is short of a quorum for a meeting of the easily-bored club – which generally takes the form of a private knockabout away from the others. In Australia at least, this was accepted as a necessary safety valve for long-standing tourists.

The various stomach problems were an early reminder of what a tour to the sub-continent can be about, and West Indies captain Viv Richards reckons that the World Cup could well hinge on which team stays fittest. On Bob Willis' tour here, the England batting order for a match at Faisalabad was entirely dependent on who was not in the lavatory at the fall of the next wicket.

Stewart has first-hand experience. His only tour here as a player, in 1963-64, ended prematurely with a bout of dysentery. He was not too worried about yesterday's disjointed workout. "It was only ever going to be a light session," he said, but he is clearly hoping for a more substantial roll-call in Rawalpindi tomorrow afternoon. The practice was originally scheduled for this morning, but after yesterday's gruelling 10-hour trip from Delhi, the management decided to allow for extra recovery time.

The trip itself involved two flights, preceded by the usual avalanche of red tape (there are close on a billion people in India, the majority of whom appear to be employed handing out forms to fill in) and followed by long waits at both Lahore and Islamabad airports, and the usual hiatus surrounding mislaid luggage.

Imran Khan was the last of the World Cup players to arrive yesterday, and the Pakistani captain's absence from the opening World Cup ceremony and friendly match against India in Delhi cost him a Japanese car. A benevolent sponsor had planned to give one each to Imran and Sunil Gavaskar for services rendered to their countries but while Sunny got his Sunny – or something similar – Imran's went back to the showroom.

A proposal that umpires use pocket television sets before making decisions has been rejected by the umpires. Dickie Bird said: "The electronic gadgets take away a lot from the umpire. They cannot help you with leg-before-wicket, bat-and-pad catches or even caught behind decisions, for one has to take a lot of things into consideration."

DATELINE RAWALPINDI, 3/10/87, MARTIN JOHNSON REPORTS...

England stand their ground over switch

England will get out into the middle for the first time on Monday for a 50-over practice match under World Cup rules in Rawalpindi. The opposition are entitled a (as opposed the *the*) Prime Minister's XI – possibly because of the unpredictability of local politics. The ground is about a mile from the jail where the previous incumbent was hung.

On Monday week, England meet Pakistan in their second Group B match at Rawalpindi, and a crowd of 20,000 is expected. The capacity appears to be around 1,500, maybe 1,750 as some of the tickets are printed: "Pavilion End Tree, Bough A."

However, while it was difficult yesterday to imagine a Lord's-sized attendance at an Ashby-de-la-Zouch sized venue, Rawalpindi has managed it before and will doubtless do so again. Besides, according to one club official's estimate, a 20,000 crowd will still leave around 30,000 potential customers without tickets.

A lot of work has to be done to get the ground ready, so much so that the local cricket association secretary wanted England to shift their practice match elsewhere. Quite where, they weren't sure. England's management, therefore, declined, and so this Monday's game will take place to the backdrop of drills, hammers, and various other destructionary noises.

Whether the actual playing area will be fit for a World Cup match by Monday week also looked dubious yesterday. It was difficult to know

Painting a boundary rope at Rawalpindi.

whether the roped-off area was to protect the square or the outfield, as both had the appearance of a farmer's field ready for stubble burning.

Still, the groundsman will have any amount of volunteer labour to call upon while he gets on with the pitch, and if that turns out to be as good as the two cut on the outfield for net practice yesterday, there won't be much wrong with it.

Everyone except Derek Pringle, confined to his hotel room with you-know-what, took part, although Eddie Hemmings possibly shouldn't have. He'd been ill all night, but decided that some kind of exercise other than sprinting from bed to bathroom would do him good, and even though he looked ghastly afterwards, said he felt "OK".

John Emburey's ankle sprain had improved sufficiently for him to bowl a few overs off a minimal run up, but the quicker bowlers all steamed in, and Phillip DeFreitas and Paul Jarvis looked particularly impressive.

If everyone is fit, everyone will play on Monday. Eleven for the tourists and the other three making up an opposition team who will probably be around Minor Counties standard.

On Wednesday another 50-over match has been arranged against an "International XI" in Lahore, which is England's base for Friday's opening

World Cup match against the West Indies – a 75-minute coach ride away in Gujranwala.

Chetan Sharma, the medium-pace bowler, has chipped a bone in his left thumb and will miss India's remaining World Cup warm-up games. Sharma, whose hand is in plaster after an operation, was injured fielding his own bowling in the World Cup charity match against Pakistan in New Delhi on Wednesday.

DATELINE ISLAMABAD, 5 /10 /87, MARTIN JOHNSON REPORTS . . .

England try to appear full of beans

England's World Cup army having thus far spent more time clutching its stomach than marching on it, the chicken tikka has been taken temporarily off the menu. During today's first full-scale practice game in Rawalpindi, the boys will be lunching on the more homely delights of Spam and baked beans.

Their manager Micky Stewart has "politely declined" to place an order with the home caterers, and now that the tourists' food hampers from home have at last turned up – they went missing when the team arrived in Islamabad on Thursday – the microwave oven has been transported to the visitors' dressing room to make its match debut.

The Tesco-sponsored tuck boxes are mainly of the canned and bottled variety and include vast quantities of the captain's favourite, Branston pickle.

As far as Mike Gatting is concerned a truckload of the stuff constitutes only about a week's supply, and this relief consignment was quite possibly obtained on NH prescription. It has arrived in the nick of time, too. Withdrawal symptoms were beginning to set in.

England might have thought about bringing a chef as well as a doctor out here, but as Spam and baked beans hardly represent *haute cuisine*, the physiotherapist Laurie Brown has been given the first shift with the can-opener. "I'm sure the locals won't be offended," said Brown, "but we have had sickness problems and maybe a few days of home cooking will help."

A couple of players were too ill to attend yesterday's net session: Nottingham's Chris Broad, who recorded a temperature of 101 in the shade during the night, and his county colleague Eddie Hemmings, who has been poorly ever since arriving. He is unable to keep anything down, and at this rate the Whale will return home as a tadpole.

Neither is expected to play in today's 50-over game against a Prime Minister's XI in Rawalpindi, and the definate absence of John Emburey because of his ankle injury will probably leave the side without a spinner.

England's original plan was to play all 14 of their squad (three for the opposition) but the way things are at present – both Bill Athey and Derek Pringle were suffering in practice yesterday – they may yet end up borrowing from the home team.

The PM entrusted selection of his side to the Pakistani manager Hasib Ashan, who will be in attendance today, so stand by for a hundred before lunch. Protests, that is. England, though, are assured of decent opposition, including at least three Test players in Zakir Khan, Sikander Bakht and Ashraf Ali.

Preparations for the World Cup group match here between England and Pakistan a week today are coming on, although the major activities yesterday – tree-pruning and boundary-post painting – hardly seemed high priority. The playing area itself, however, has been improved by a couple of heavy thunderstorms, and we will have a good idea of the likely quality of the pitch after today.

It would be nice by now to have a good idea of England's probable line-up for their opening group match against the West Indies in Gujwanrala on Friday – but if it were being played today it would be a straight choice of the 11 who felt the least wonky. "The fittest bloke we've got," said Stewart ruefully, "is the Doc. And he's eaten everything."

DATELINE RAWALPINDI, 6 /10 /87, MARTIN JOHNSON REPORTS . . .

Small change pays dividends

Notwithstanding the modest quality of the opposition, England looked reasonably impressive in yesterday's 53-run victory over a Prime Minister's XI here. However, whether this departure from last winter's successful formula – perform like duffers on the small occasion – bodes well for the more serious stuff ahead, only time will tell.

The official crowd estimate was 10,000 (which may or may not have included the 2,000 or so non-paying customers peering over railings and out of treetops), and the place lacked nothing in atmosphere. All it did in fact lack was a decent one-day pitch.

A shovel and a pair of stilts would have been handy batting accessories. Depending on whether the ball landed on one of the cracked, grassy patches or bare brown ones, it came through at either nostril or ankle height. Mike Gatting's pre-match estimate of a winning 50-over total was 170, and he was about right.

Bough A, Branch 4: 250 rupees.

England would probably have made comfortably in excess of 200 had they not generously donated Gladstone Small to the opposition. Small's first delivery flew off a length past Tim Robinson's visor, and even after his own on-the-spot decision to throttle back by at least a couple of yards in pace, Small dismissed England's three major stroke-players, Graham Gooch, Allan Lamb and Gatting, in his 10-over spell with the new ball. Small may soon get a game for England.

Despite the fact that the pitch was at its most unpredictable for the first hour-and-a-half, Small's performance did highlight the potentially embarrassing position in which England may find themselves. As soon as the World Cup is over, assuming Graham Dilley has proved his fitness, Small is booked on the plane back to Heathrow. The Warwickshire sea-mer, who left the field immediately after completing his spell to discover he had been locked out of the England dressing-room by way of retribution, looks encouragingly fit after last summer's side-strain problems. He has been one of the few tourists so far to discover that room with a view on the sub-continent does not necessarily mean a picture of the Taj Mahal on the lavatory wall.

All things considered (the microwave lunch, by the way, went down well and stayed down), it was an achievement for England to get 12 fit men on parade, although one example of forward planning is the provision of sanitary towels. To be worn back to front, inside the flannels, in case of accidents. During a lunchtime stroll around Rawalpindi – more of a nervous dart than a stroll, actually, because of the total absence of anything resembling the Highway Code – a pedestrian approached one of our number with the inquiry: "No Iron Bottom?" Except for a fortunate few, unhappily not.

In addition to his three wickets, Small also greeted Gatting with a first-ball thud into the midriff which might have felled many a lesser stomach. Once Small was out of sight, however, batting was altogether easier.

Robinson won the man-of-the-match award for an unimpressive 46, although Paul Downton was a worthier candidate. Then, towards the end of the innings, the jerry-built TV gantry, which bobbled around all day like an unset jelly, somehow survived two encounters with Neil Foster sixes.

All five bowlers took wickets – Phillip DeFreitas three in a spell of four balls – but he lost his length and direction in his later overs, and Derek Pringle probably moved ahead of him on points in the all-rounder stakes.

Both DeFreitas and Eddie Hemmings (twice) were struck for sixes by the PM's No. 9 Sabih Azhar during a last-wicket partnership of 44. Given the difficulties in adjusting to the diet and climate during this first week, England's attack probably performed as well as could have been expected. However, if the pitch is as up-and-down as this one for next Monday's World Cup clash against Pakistan, yesterday's form will by no means be good enough.

RAWALPINDI SCOREBOARD

ENGLAND

G A Gooch b Small 2
R T Robinson c Masoud b Naveed 46
*M W Gatting b Small 7
A J Lamb c Shaukat b Small 12
C W J Athey lbw b Naveed 11
D R Pringle c Ashraf b Shakil 24
#P R Downton b Nadeem 50
P A DeFreitas lbw b Nadeem 0
N A Foster not out 25
P W Jarvis b Nadeem 1
E E Hemmings not out 3
Extras (b1, lb8, nb2, w1) 12
Total (for 9, 50 overs) 193

Fall of wickets: 1-4, 2-18, 3-48, 4-76, 5-91, 6-143, 7-148, 8-183, 9-187.

Bowling: Zakir Khan 10-2-35-0; Small 10-2-30-3; Akram Raza 8-1-18-0; Naveed Anjum 10-2-38-2; Shakil Ahmed 5-0-33-1; Nadeem Ghauri 5-0-17-3; Zahid Ahmed 2-0-13-0.

ENGLAND WON BY 53 RUNS

PRIME MINISTER'S XI

Masoud Anwar c Lamb b Jarvis 1
Amir Sohail c Downton b Foster 21
Mansoor Rana c Gooch b Pringle 26
Shaukat Mirza c Gatting b Foster 4
Zahid Ahmad c and b DeFreitas 1
Naveed Anjum c Foster b DeFreitas 0
Ashraf Ali c Downton b DeFreitas 0
Akram Raza c Foster b Hemmings 11
Sabih Azhar not out 57
Zakir Khan run out 1
Shakil Ahmad b Hemmings 2
Extras (b7, lb1, w7, nb1) 16
Total (36.3 overs) 140

Fall of wickets: 1-7, 2-47, 3-58, 4-58, 5-61, 6-61, 7-62, 8-84, 9-96.

Bowling: Jarvis 10-1-39-1, Foster 6-0-25-2, Pringle 5-3-3-1, DeFreitas 7-1-30-3, Hemmings 8.3-2-35-3.

Stewart warns the whingers

Forty-eight hours before England take on the West Indies in their opening Group B World Cup match, an outbreak of what might conceivably be described as Delhi bellyache has broken out in the camp – and treatment is currently being administered by the team manager as opposed to the tour doctor.

As any Australian will tell you, we are already world champions when it comes to whingeing, and opportunities for a good moan tend to come along more frequently than usual in the sub-continent. Yesterday, however, Micky Stewart was wearing his stern hat for the first time when he delivered a "cut out the complaining and get on with some work" sermon to his players.

While conceding that there had been some grounds for long faces because of stomach ailments, heat, travel and dodgy playing conditions, Stewart said: "I've told them to stop worrying and put in a bit of hard graft. If we want to win this thing we must start thinking more positively."

He was particularly concerned to hear one or two players grumbling about the ground at Rawalpindi, where England played their first practice game two days ago, and the venue for their second World Cup match against Pakistan on Monday. The nub of it, apparently, is that the square itself is wretchedly uneven, and fielding on the outfield is an exercise not to be undertaken without a box, gumshield, and possibly a prayer or two.

While those sentiments are not without some justification, the England management are concerned that the players might develop a complex about the place. This would by no means be without precedent. If you want to see an English Test batsman leap six feet into the air try sneaking up behind him and whispering "Headingley" into his ear.

Neither has the fact that Pakistan's two group games against the West Indies are both being played at Test centres – Karachi and Lahore – been allowed to pass without the odd sarcastic comment. Karachi is likely to be a slow turner and Lahore flat – either way, not made to measure for the West Indian quicks.

That sort of careful selection, though, was only to be expected, and as ideas go it's not exactly a trail-blazer. You may recall football's World Cup in 1966 when England, by some happy coincidence, found themselves at Wembley for every game.

At least England now have a good idea of what to expect in Rawalpindi, which may not be the case for Friday's match in Gujranwala. It's 50 miles from the team's base in Lahore and while Stewart plans to take a look at the ground tomorrow, the players won't be seeing it until a couple of hours before the start.

England, meantime, should offer some indication of whether they have absorbed the manager's "grit the teeth" message when they meet an Invitation XI here today. They include both the players who missed the other warm-up game on Monday because of illness and injury respectively, Chris Broad and John Emburey.

The England and West Indies teams are both staying at the Hilton International in Lahore, although the most celebrated guest at the moment – in an executive suite originally reserved for tour manager Peter Lush, and on the same floor as the Press and players – is Muhammad Ali.

Judging by the traffic jam in the corridor caused by room service trollies, the 45-year-old former boxing champion – here at General Zia's invitation – has not lost his appetite. Sadly, however, the power of speech largely appears to have deserted him. Even sadder, what were once the fleetest legs in his business now get him around at what amounts to no more than a shuffle, and the old flashing eyes have become an impenetrable blank.

DATELINE LAHORE, 8 /10 /87, MARTIN JOHNSON REPORTS . . .

Jarvis on alert at the England side door

England concluded their World Cup warm-up programme yesterday with a routine 129-run victory over a team of local weekend cricketers. The microwave heroes may be here in terms of the luncheon interval, but as far as preparations for the West Indies tomorrow were concerned it was a bit like training for the Olympic 1500 metres by walking the dog around the block.

The players themselves would have much preferred something tougher (although pen moaning has been officially banned), and it did at least provide further experience of the feeling of playing inside an incinerator. On top of that, all the front-line batsmen have now had a decent knock. In many ways it was more an exercise in PR than competitive cricket. England agreed to lose the toss and be inserted because the Chief Minister of the Punjab, down to open his team's batting, couldn't get off work until lunchtime. He made one, which was one better than he made against the West Indies last week.

Refreshments at Lahore Gymkhana.

As a reciprocal gesture, the host club presented each member of the England squad (including the Doc) with a woollen carpet. Not the flying kind, unfortunately, so they're still stuck with the lotteries known as PIA and Air India.

The ceremony, by the way, in keeping with the feeling that the cricket was largely incidental, took place halfway through the home innings.

It was therapeutic merely to be at the Gymkhana Ground yesterday. It is as green and picturesque as any in England – a little like Queen's Park, Chesterfield, in fact – and, unlike Rawalpindi, the pitch was a belter. Pakistan twice used it for international matches in the Fifties, although heaven knows how they controlled the crowd, but the Gadaffi Stadium just down the road is now Lahore's regular Test venue.

England yesterday provided a sizeable clue as to the identity of their final XI for tomorrow's match in Gujranwala when Eddie Hemmings, Paul Jarvis and Bill Athey all guested for the opposition. It is fair to deduce from this, particularly in view of the fact that Athey didn't score heavily enough to claim the place earmarked for Tim Robinson, that those will be the three players omitted. Jarvis, though, may still get in through the side door because of a slight doubt about Phillip DeFreitas. He delivered a number of sick notes under curious circumstances to his Leicestershire captain Peter Willey last summer, but it's unlikely that "hurt shoulder during a bout of coughing" was among them. DeFreitas has contrived to pull some shoulder ligaments in this way. He and Gladstone Small are pencilled in to open the bowling (DeFreitas's record in four World Series matches against the West Indies last winter, incidentally, was eight wickets at two runs an over) but if he doesn't make it Neil Foster will get the new ball instead.

Graham Gooch, Chris Broad, Mike Gatting and Allan Lamb all got runs, the first two retiring to give others a go, and a wicket didn't actually fall until Gatting was out at 215 in the 45th over. John Emburey bowled well enough to suggest that he is now over his ankle strain, and it was the vice-captain who dismissed Athey for 29. Athey thin-edged a cut giving Emburey the charge, but there are sufficient doubts about the umpiring in this World Cup for Paul Downton to have stumped him as well, just in case.

England will be happy enough to have the Australian Tony Crafter in charge of three of their group matches, but both Crafter and Dickie Bird have experienced problems lately. Crafter arrived in Lahore to find himself without a hotel room, while Bird went for an early-morning stroll on the beach in Madras and waded into some untreated sewage. Dickie, so health-conscious he would faint at the thought of an ice cube in his drink out here, does have a hotel room, and is reported to have locked himself in it.

The manager, Micky Stewart, took himself off to Gujranwala to check on facilities for the Windies game, but at least crowd trouble should not be a major problem in England's group. The authorities are, however, worried about India's games at Nagpur and Ahmedabad, both of which have previous convictions. At a Test in Ahmedabad last March Pakistan – who launch the Cup against Sri Lanka in Hyderabad today - were pelted with stones and other sharp objects. England would settle for fruit which, someone opined, is sold with a "throw-by" date stamped on it here.

LAHORE GYMKHANA CLUB SCOREBOARD

ENGLAND
G A Gooch retired	68
B C Broad retired	67
*M W Gatting c Bhinder b Asim	43
A J Lamb st Hayee b Asim	34
J E Emburey b Asim	11
P A J DeFreitas not out	17
D R Pringle not out	6
Extras (b 2, lb 8, w 6, nb 4)	15
Total (for 3, 50 overs)	**261**

Fall of wickets: 1-215, 2-230, 3-249.
Bowling: Jarvis 10-2-43-0, Bhinder 10-0-51-0, Nasrullah 3-1-13-0, Zaman 5-0-34-0, Zulfiqar 7-0-31-0, Hemmings 10-0-52-0, Asim 5-0-32-3.

ENGLAND WON BY 129 RUNS

LAHORE CLUB XI
Jamil Rana c Gatting b Pringle	17
Nawaz Sherif b DeFreitas	1
Salman Ahmad retired	24
C W J Athey c Downton b Emburey	29
Zaee Qadri c Downton b Small	0
Bilal lbw Gatting	10
Hammad Khan not out	26
Mohammed Nawaz b Emburey	11
E E Hemmings not out	5
Extras (lb 5, w 1, nb 3)	9
Total (for 6, 50 overs)	**132**

Fall of wickets: 1-5, 2-24, 3-76, 4-77, 5-97, 6-125.
Bowling: DeFreitas 2-1-2-1-; Foster 10-2-16-0; Small 9-2-21-1; Pringle 9-3-10-1; Gooch 5-0-20-0; Emburey 9-2-37-2; Gatting 6-0-21-1.

Dean Jones scored 65 in Australia's final warm-up match before they meet India in the World Cup tomorrow. The Australians hit 259 for 9 in 50 overs, and then dismissed an Indian South Zone team for 161 in 49 overs to win by 98 runs.

Chetan Sharma will miss India's first two games after chipping a thumb bone.

DATELINE MADRAS, 9/10/87, HENRY BLOFELD REPORTS . . .

Concrete and courtesy

India is never slow to show both sides of its face. I had barely dropped off to sleep at 1am in Delhi's airport hotel, anticipating a wake-up call in $3\frac{1}{2}$ hours' time, when a loud knock on the door revealed an enthusiastic porter determined to deliver someone else's luggage.

When I pointed out somewhat tersely that it was the wrong room, he smiled so disarmingly that I was almost made to feel guilty myself. Back at the airport an hour later, most of the population of the country seemed to be trying to catch the same flight to Hyderabad and Madras, but with unfailing charm and courtesy.

Madras is hot, sticky and delightful and if all roads do not exactly lead to the Chepauk Stadium – the buses are on strike – the World Cup is everyone's topic of conversation. Even the latest atrocities of the Tamil Tigers on Sri Lanka have been relegated to second place. As always, the taxi drivers pack a year's excitement into a journey of two miles.

The newspapers are devoting endless space to the cricket. Yesterday morning, before a ball has been bowled, *The Times of India* ran 14 cricket stories, including a despatch from London saying that The Oval may be forced to close down. It was a mystery, though, as to why Clive Lloyd should have written a lengthy preview of New Zealand's chances.

Chepauk, which incidentally staged the first Ranju Trophy match, has become a concrete giant, but has certainly produced its share of drama. It was here a year ago that India and Australia played only the second tie in Test history.

Andy Roberts, for the West Indies, and Neil Foster, for England, have won Test matches on this ground, where fast bowlers seem to enjoy themselves nowadays. In 1976-77, John Lever was accused by the umpire and all of India of using Vaseline to shine the ball. He had stuck strips of impregnated gauze just above his eyebrows to prevent sweat running into his eyes and it needed all Tony Greig's diplomatic skills as captain to avert the attentions of the Indian media at one of the more famous of rest-day press conferences.

Today's opening match in Group A between India, the favourites to win the group, and Australia, on a pitch which looked full of runs yesterday, promises to be hard fought. India, as the world champions, will be anxious to start with a victory before an expected 50,000 spectators, while an early success would do wonders for Australian confidence. India's depth of batting could provide the answer.

Madras has its habitual water shortage and the former Indian off-spinner Venkat, who is the secretary at Chepauk, has been buying a dozen lorryloads of water each day for the last fortnight. The condition of the ground is surprisingly good, despite the drought, but the forecast has a familiar ring to English ears. Rain fell for a time yesterday and is still hanging around.

Two former England captains, Bob Willis and Mike Smith, are now on opposite sides in the dispute at Warwickshire following yesterday's resignation of Willis from the club's general committee.

Willis is likely to join forces with the members who forced a special meeting on 11 November to debate a "no confidence" vote in the chairman and committee. Smith took over the chair on Wednesday after Tony Steven stepped down, but the root of Willis's discontent lies with the "management style" of the general secretary, David Heath.

DATELINE, 9/10/87, MARTIN JOHNSON REPORTS . . .

PAKISTAN v SRI LANKA
Sri Lankans improvise a warning

England, who scarcely needed any extra evidence that theirs is much the tougher of the two World Cup groups, received it anyway yesterday with the result of the opening match in Hyderabad.

Sri Lanka, chasing a daunting 268 to beat Pakistan, the tournament favourites, lost by only 15 runs, and as suspected, look fully capable of throwing a spanner into anyone's works. Looking at it positively, however, at least the Doc won't have to dip into his bag for overconfidence pills before England meet them at Peshawar and Pune.

You wouldn't back to the Sri Lankans to contain anyone to much below 250 but their batsmen possess remarkably nimble footwork (but then you need to have in a country that records 100 deaths a year from falling coconuts), have all the improvisation needed for one-day cricket and not many totals will be out of their reach.

They were favourites to win at one stage yesterday, needing 88 of the final 15 overs with six wickets in hand. But if their batting is vulnerable anywhere though, it's probably in over-excitability, and what eventually did for them was losing their two top scorers, Mahanama and De Silva, in quick succession to a long-hop and full-toss respectively.

Abdul Qadir spun the odd ball sharply but the Sri Lankans dismembered Pakistan's most successful one-day bowler Mudassar (9-0-63-0) and on that basis – plus the fact that England's batsmen may well faint at the sight of him – one of last summer's two mirages, (the other was the sun), Saleem Jaffer could well be recalled for Monday's game at Peshawar.

Interestingly enough, Pakistan knocked an early hole in the theory that 9am starts would produce a rash of insertions by opting to bat first, and it was almost inevitable that Javed Miandad would score the competition's inaugural century.

Javed, who may already have more cash in his account than the bank he works for has in its vaults, doubtless came in for another avalanche of sponsored rupees – and we almost saw more of him in the inter-over commercials on TV than in the game itself.

While Javed, apparently, scores all his runs because he uses Lifebuoy soap, Wasim Akram takes all his wickets by drinking tinned instant milk. The ads come thick and fast and the Beeb will have to be on the ball if they're not to reintroduce cigarette advertising inadvertently to our screens. The message to armchair punters here, (and it comes about every third ball), is that you can't possibly enjoy the game without puffing non stop on a Wills Filter Tip.

At least we'll have our own commentators, which is a blessing. Sample dialogue yesterday. Poser for expert: "Pakistan must be grateful for so many extras." Expert: "Yes, they've had a lot of extras." The camerawork, though, appears perfectly adequate, even if the director appears to be under orders to greet each Pakistani boundary with a shot of the Prime Minister beaming from the VIP box.

The odds on Pakistan winning Group B, while certainly advanced by the drawing of early blood, probably have more to do with a carefully orchestrated itinerary. Their three opponents face at least one flight every five days, flitting around between the foot of the Khyber Pass (Peshawar) to the east of Bombay (Pune). Pakistan, on the other hand, don't have to leave their own country.

We will have a clearer idea of England's prospects after their own opening match against the West Indies today in Gujranwala, a venue inspected yesterday by manager Micky Stewart, and pronounced "brilliant" both in terms of facilities and playing conditions.

England's batsmen look in good form, but today it is Walsh, Gray, Patterson etc on a pitch that Stewart expected to offer extra bounce. This could make Chris Broad a highly influential figure, and there was an amusing indication of just how much the Nottinghamshire opening batsman has grown in world stature since last winter during England's second practice match in Lahore on Wednesday. "Who," enquired one local spectator, "is that batting with Chris Broad?" It was, as it happens, Graham Gooch. Last night England still didn't know whether Phillip DeFreitas would be fit to play, although as he bowled only three deliveries – with 10 minutes break in between each – Stewart conceded that an "overnight miracle" was necessary.

DeFreitas injured his shoulder tendons during a coughing fit, unusual but by no means a record in terms of odd injuries. Derek Pringle once ricked his back when he was writing a letter, and a former England rugby player suffered a similar fate pushing away a plate of apple pie. "At least," someone who knows about the skipper's fondness for second helpings remarked, "that could never happen to Gatt."

HYDERABAD SCOREBOARD

PAKISTAN

Rameez Raja c R J Ratnayake b Anurasiri 76
Ejaz Ahmed c Kuruppu b R J Ratnayake 16
Mansoor Akhtar c R J Ratnayake
                     b J R Ratnayake 12
Javed Miandad b J R Ratnayake 103
Wasim Akram run out 14
Salim Malik not out 18
*Imran Khan b R J Ratnayake 2
#Salim Yousuf not out 1
Extras (lb 15, nb 1, w 9) 25
Total (for 6, 50 overs) 267

Fall of wickets: 1-48, 2-67, 3-180, 4-226, 5-259, 6-266.
Did not bat: Abdul Qadir, Mudassar Nazar, Tauseef Ahmed.
Bowling: John 10-2-37-0; R J Ratnayake 10-0-64-2; J R Ratnayake 9-0-47-2; De Silva 10-0-44-0; Anurasiri 10-0-52-1; Gurusingha 1-0-8-0.

PAKISTAN WON BY 15 RUNS

SRI LANKA

#B Kurrupu c Yousuf b Imran 9
R Mahanama c Miandad b Mansoor Akhtar .. 89
R Dias b Qadir....................... 5
A Ranatunga b Tauseef 24
*D Mendis run out 1
A Gurusingha b Qadir 37
A De Silva b Imran 42
J R Ratnayake c Yousuf b Akram 7
R J Ratnayake c Mudassar b Akram 8
V John not out 1
D Anurasiri run out 0
Extras (b 7, lb 14, nb 1, w 7) 29
Total (all out, 49.2 overs)............. 252

Fall of wickets: 1-29, 2-57, 3-100, 4-103, 5-182, 6-190, 7-209, 8-223, 9-251.
Bowling: Imran 10-2-42-2; Akram 9.2-1-41-2; Mudassar 9-0-63-0; Qadir 10-1-30-2; Tauseef 10-0-48-1; Mansoor Akhtar 1-0-7-1.

ENGLAND v WEST INDIES

Lamb leads revivalist movement

For more than a decade it has been an achievement for an England batsman to hang on to his teeth, never mind his wicket, against the West Indies attack. So if the Caribbean bubble has finally burst, it's rather a nice feeling that we should have been the ones wielding the pin.

In the sauna bath heat of Gujranwala yesterday, England not only launched their World Cup challenge with one of the great limited-over international victories, but also made it five wins out of the last six against opposition that not so long ago were regarded as nigh on invincible. Suddenly we have the West Indian sign on them.

It has long been thought that if ever the West Indies were deprived of their major weapon – the throat ball – and were obliged to bowl at the stumps instead, things might be different.

Yesterday, with the bouncer effectively outlawed by the shoulder-height no-ball rule, England – just as they did in the World Series Challenge in Australia – demonstrated the difference between being confronted by a sharp row of teeth and a set of dentures.

In the end, without minimising the contributions lower down the order, it was Allan Lamb who won an improbable victory by two wickets

John Emburey runs out Desmond Haynes.

Clyde Best is comprehensively bowled by DeFreitas for five.

with three balls to spare, in circumstances that brought back memories of his 18 off Bruce Reid's final over under the SCG lights last winter.

This time it was Courtney Walsh who got the treatment – although, from the tour doctor, so did Lamb. Not surprisingly, in temperatures over 100 degrees, he was badly dehydrated and had to be helped back out of the dressing-room to collect his man-of-the-match medal.

It seemed ironic that England's apparent collapse from 98 for 2, when they were making comfortable progress towards their target of 244, should have been precipitated not by one of the West Indians' fast bowlers, but by an inexperienced 20-year-old from Guyana, bowling at around Barry Wood's pace, only without his swing or seam.

It seemed apt, too, that Carl Hooper should have struck shortly after the local mullah had mercifully finished three and half hours of non-stop incantation through the quadraphonic loud-speakers on top of the town mosque. After Mike Gatting and Graham Gooch had fallen in the space of four balls from Hooper, England, one felt, hadn't a prayer left either.

Gatting, who outsmarted himself with some nifty footwork and ended up missing a straight one, and Gooch, who edged a half-wide volley, had put on 58 in nine overs, and with Hooper also removing Derek Pringle, England apparently reached a low point at 131 for 6 from 37 overs. One observer refused to accept that prognosis, offering as his argument the fact that Pringle had by then removed himself from the match.

A shade unkind, but it wasn't one of Pringle's better days. His 12 runs took him eight overs, he'd apparently spent the previous night perusing the Colin Milburn pocket guide to fielding, and his bowling was annihilated.

From the moment Viv Richards clouted his second and third deliveries for four, Pringle lost it completely and ended up with the most expensive analysis from an England bowler in a one-day international.

Until he came on as England's fifth bowler, John Emburey and Phillip DeFreitas had kept the West Indies reasonably well contained on a pitch that, while dotted with shaving-brush-like tufts of grass, behaved impeccably.

However, the West Indies scored 84 runs off their last eight overs and, well though Gus Logie and Roger Harper played, Neil Foster was smashed because he lost totally his hitherto perfect length, and Pringle because he never found a length to lose in the first place. His final over, including one huge six from Harper, cost 22.

England's innings followed a similar course – a little like a sandwich with nothing in the middle. In fact, when Emburey came in at 136 Lamb had not only done precious little, but had also just run out the in-form Paul Downton.

John Emburey is bowled by Patterson having a conventional 'slog'.

England needed an improbable 91 from their final 10 overs – although the West Indies made 92 from theirs – and it was Emburey who got the momentum going. They've probably never seen anything quite like him in Gujranwala, but one sight of his patent-pending off-balance flat-bat pull that flies straight into the sight screen for six (off Patterson) was enough to send them into raptures.

He was bowled next ball having – by comparison – an orthodox slog but DeFreitas, suitably infected, made a dashing 23 in five overs and Lamb was finally beginning to motor.

Even so, 35 off the last three overs with two wickets left seemed highly unlikely until Lamb (who had been in for 18 overs without a boundary before hitting a four and six in Walsh's eighth over) then plundered 16 runs off his ninth. The penultimate over from Patterson yielded only six, but with 13 required off the last, Walsh blew a terminal gasket.

A full toss that Lamb put away for four was followed by four wides down the leg side and a no-ball. Foster then squirted the winning boundary down to third man, and the West Indies' senior bowler, after purveying his first five overs for 11, tottered off in tears having gone for 31 off his final nine legitimate deliveries.

Lamb tottered off too, and confessed later that he'd ended up playing entirely from memory. Poor old Walsh, however, won't have felt like tying a knot in this particular handkerchief.

Lamb said: "It was not a one-man victory. Everyone chipped in at the end, and everyone played their part. Embers, Daffy and Fossie took the pressure off me a bit, and were full of encouragement. I was enjoying it but I haven't played in heat like that for a long time. And I don't think I could have lasted another over."

GUJRANWALA SCOREBOARD

WEST INDIES

D L Haynes run out	19
C A Best b DeFreitas	5
R B Richardson b Foster	53
*I V Richards b Foster	27
#P J Dujon run out	46
A L Logie b Foster	49
R A Harper b Small	24
C L Hooper not out	1
W K M Benjamin not out	7
Extras (lb 9, nb 3)	12
Total (7 wkts, 50 overs)	**243**

Fall of wickets: 1-8, 2-53, 3-105, 4-122, 5-205, 6-235, 7-235.

Did not bat: C A Walsh, B P Patterson.

Bowling: DeFreitas 10-2-31-1; Foster 10-0-53-3; Emburey 10-2-22-0; Small 10-0-45-1; Pringle 10-0-83-2.

ENGLAND WON BY 2 WICKETS

ENGLAND

B C Broad c Dujon b Walsh	3
G A Gooch c Dujon b Hooper	47
R T Robinson run out	12
*M W Gatting b Hooper	25
A J Lamb not out	67
D R Pringle c Best b Hooper	12
#P R Downton run out	3
J E Emburey b Patterson	22
P A J DeFreitas b Patterson	23
N A Foster not out	9
Extras (lb 14, w 6, nb 3)	23
Total (for 8, 49.3 overs)	**246**

Fall of wickets: 1-14, 2-40, 3-98, 4-99, 5-123, 6-131, 7-162, 8-209.

Did not bat: G Small

Bowling: Patterson 10-0-49-2; Walsh 9.3-0-65-1; Harper 10-0-44-0; Benjamin 10-1-32-0; Hooper 10-0-42-3.

Roasted Lamb: Physio Laurie Brown helps a dehydrated Allan Lamb off the field.

A jubilant Gatting said: "It's nice to see the lads haven't lost their taste for winning. I always thought we were in with a chance as long as Allan was there. He was magnificent and got us out of trouble yet again when we were in a tight corner. But it was a good team effort, and this win should help everyone."

DATELINE MADRAS, 10/10/87, HENRY BLOFELD REPORTS ...

INDIA v AUSTRALIA

Australia enjoy the last resort

If anything, the World Cup produced an even more remarkable game in Madras than it had in Gujranwala. With one ball left Steve Waugh knocked out Maninder Singh's off stump and Australia had beaten India, the World Cup holders, by one run with one ball to spare.

Australia were put in to bat on a belter of a pitch for the simple reason that with a 9 o'clock start the outfield was still damp with dew and therefore slow. They were given a great start by David Boon and Geoff Marsh who put on 110 in 25 overs for the first wicket and they went on the pass 200 in the 40th over with only two wickets down.

The middle order then lost their way and Australia finished at 270 for 6 when they should at least have reached 300. As it was, a total of 270 was at once made to look inadequate when India were given an even more astonishing start by Sunil Gavaskar and Kris Srikkanth.

Gavaskar hit six fours and one six in an extraordinary first 12 overs and even outscored Srikkanth. They put on 69 before Gavaskar hit Peter Taylor to deep mid-off. By then, Craig McDermott's first four overs had cost 31 runs and Bruce Reid's fourth went for 11.

It was phenomenal stroke-play and Allan Border did well to hold his side together, the fielding was most impressive. Gavaskar's backfoot drive off McDermott in the first over of the innings which went straight for four was the stroke of the year. The drive which sent off-spinner Taylor's first ball straight over mid off was not far behind.

After Gavaskar had gone 24-year-old Navjot Siddhu came out to play a fine innings in his first one-day international. He played his first two overs thoughtfully whilst Srikkanth took over the assault from Gavaskar.

Then, in his third he came down the pitch and straight drove Taylor for six which hardly portrays a nervous temperament. After that he produced a series of wonderful strokes and the only blemish on his batting was an apparent determination to run out either his partner or himself or maybe both.

He and Srikkanth put on 52 for the second wicket before Srikkanth was lbw pulling at Waugh. Dilip Vengsarkar, not at his best, joined Siddhu and added 76 most of which came to Siddhu in 11 overs. Siddhu's final assault included two driven sixes off Taylor and a drive and a pull off Border and two more before he was yorked by McDermott.

After that the Indians panicked. There was no real urgency but Mohammad Azharuddin, at his worst, swung wildly and lost his middle stump. Vengsarkar heaved crudely to wide mid-on, Ravi Shastri pushed back a simple return catch, Kapil Dev, nowhere near his best either, drove into mid-wicket's stomach, Roger Binney was thrown out wastefully and so also was Monoj Prabhakar.

Australia need congratulating for sticking to their job when things were going so badly. In the final stages Reid again bowled extremely well – his first three overs had given away only one run – and he and McDermott showed there is no substitute for line and length.

So to the last over when six were needed from six balls. Maninder, who was better than his best for four balls, turned Waugh to long leg for two, pushed defensively at the second ball and then steered him to third man for two more and two were therefore needed from the last three balls. The fourth was blocked, and Maninder swung at the fifth and down went his off-stump.

It had been a wonderful spicy day which had almost smelt of hot curry.

MADRAS SCOREBOARD

AUSTRALIA

D C Boon lbw Shastri 49
G R Marsh c Azharuddin b Prabhakar 110
D M Jones c Sidhu b Maninder 39
*A R Border b Binny 16
T W Moody c Kapil Dev b Prabhakar 8
S R Waugh not out 19
S P O'Donnell run out 7
Extras (lb 18, w 2, nb 2) 22
Total (6 wkts, 50 overs) 270

Fall of wickets: 1-110, 2-174, 3-228, 4-237, 5-251, 6-270.
Did not bat: #G C Dyer, P R Taylor, C J McDermott, and B A Reid.
Bowling: Kapil Dev 10-0-41-0; Prabhakar 10-0-47-2; Binny 7-0-46-1; Maninder Singh 10-0-48-1; Shastri 10-0-50-1; Azharuddin 3-0-20-0.

AUSTRALIA WON BY 1 RUN

INDIA

S M Gavaskar c Reid b Taylor 37
K Srikkanth lbw Waugh 70
N Sidhu b McDermott 73
D B Vengsarkar c Jones b McDermott 29
M Azharuddin b McDermott 10
*Kapil Dev c Boon b O'Donnel 6
R J Shastri c and b McDermott 12
#K S More not out 12
R M H Binney run out 0
M Prabhakar run out 5
Maninder Singh b Waugh 4
Extras (lb 7, b 2, w 2) 11
Total (49.5 overs) 269

Fall of wickets: 1-69, 2-131, 3-207, 4-229, 5-232, 6-246, 7-256, 8-256, 9-265.
Bowling: McDermott 10-0-56-4; Reid 10-2-35-0; O'Donnell 9-1-32-1; Taylor 5-0-46-1; Waugh 9.5-0-52-2; Border 6-0-39-0.

Gatting glosses over the gaps

There aren't many places in Pakistan at this time of year in which parasols double up as umbrellas, but Islamabad, the custom-built Legoland capital, and its twin city Rawalpindi, are certainly among them. Outside the monsoon season, they represent the sub-continent's equivalent of Manchester.

England's flight from Lahore for today's match against Pakistan in Rawalpindi was as hairy for the players in economy class as it was for the BBC in first (keep your eye on the licence fee) as splashdown came down at the back end of a 15-hour electrical storm that sounded as though it might have called in on southern England on the way.

According to local newspaper reports crops have been flooded, trees felled and traffic disrupted – although the latter is a decidedly relative term here in dodgem city, where to cross the road using the Green Cross Code is the quickest way to get acquainted with the Red Cross Code. As far as the cricket goes, the rain washed away projected net practice and also threw up the possibility of that peculiarly English result – match abandoned, two points each.

More rain of the cat and dog variety fell last night, and while World Cup rules allow for a reduced contest of a minimum 25 overs per side, if necessary, the England captain Mike Gatting would prefer to utilise tomorrow's extra day and play the full 50.

One thing is rigid. If a start is made on the first day of a game, and rain strikes after even one delivery, there is no carry-over. The pitch at least has been kept dry, despite the primitive nature of the covering, which appears to be some kind of reinforced Clingfilm. Also, notwithstanding the fact that its next-door neighbour was more suitable for growing potatoes in that playing cricket on for England's practice match here last week, this one is firm, bleached white in appearance, and looks as good as the one used at Gujranwala on Friday.

England's memorable victory over the West Indies there has certainly given a psychological lift, although it has also prompted Gatting to gloss over one or two deficiencies. He pronounced the fielding "very safe", which it was if you compare it to a class of local tap-water, and put down Derek Pringle's bowling to sweaty fingers and correspondingly difficult grip. If so, it was probably peculiar – on England's side any way – to Pringle.

However, while it was probably fair enough to put Pringle's performance down to one of those gruesome off-days that afflict us all from time to time, tour captains are instinctively over-protective on these occasions, and England's decision to stick to the same team today was as predictable as it is probably incorrect.

If nothing else, this competition is too short not to get the formula right. Beating the West Indies – to some extent by default – has given England considerable latitude, and this fielding side is just not good enough to justify the exclusion of Jarvis and Athey in favour of Pringle and Robinson.

There is little doubt, though, that Gatting's adaptability on the field had a major influence on the result. He was quick to recognise that the searing heat made it extremely difficult for anyone bar John Emburey to bowl their overs in even two spells, and by judicious juggling the respective blocks of 10 overs per bowler worked out thus: DeFreitas 5-3-2; Foster 4-4-2; Emburey 5-5; Small 7-2-1; and Pringle 6-3-1.

Viv Richards, on the other hand, stuck rigidly to the painting by numbers formula: Patterson 5-5; Walsh 5-5; Harper 10; Benjamin 5-5; Hooper 10. In those crucial closing overs, when everyone else was bowled out, Patterson and Walsh appeared to be trying to run through a pit of treacle in cement clogs.

Meantime, security surrounding the World Cup matches is as tight as ever. Hyderabad was swept for mines on the morning of Pakistan's opening match against Sri Lanka, and 3,000 armed troops are reported to be on standby for England's fourth match against Pakistan in Karachi on 20 October.

Even though cricket loses just a little of its charm when the business end of a Sten-gun is tickling your nostrils at the turnstile, there is more than enough volatility in the region to make tight security both understandable and desirable.

Tight is the word. Cameras and binoculars are on the list of banned spectator articles, but there might just have been a case of overreaction at the inaugural ceremony in Delhi when a local radio commentator was turfed out for being in possession of a packet of throat lozenges.

DATELINE HYDERABAD, 12/10/87, HENRY BLOFELD REPORTS...

NEW ZEALAND v ZIMBABWE
Aussies afraid of Houghton and history

Australia, who had the humiliation of losing to Zimbabwe in the World Cup in 1983, had serious fears of a repetition on Tuesday raised by an astonishing match here.

David Houghton, the Zimbabwe wicket-keeper, played arguably the most heroic innings ever in a one-day international only to see his side fall agonisingly close to an inconceivable victory over New Zealand, who in the end won by three runs.

New Zealand had made 242 for 7, which was fewer than had seemed likely after a formidable start. But when, after 27 overs of their innings, Zimbabwe were 104 for 7 it seemed more than enough.

At this point Houghton was into the sixties – no one else had passed 12 – when he was joined by Iain Butchart, the medium-pace seam bowler. In the next 20 overs they put on 117, a record for the eighth wicket in any one-day international, before Houghton was brilliantly caught at long-on, having hit 14 off the first four balls of the 47th over.

Zimbabwe then needed 22 from 20 balls. Two run-outs tilted the balance back New Zealand's way, but after Butchart had pulled the fifth ball of the 49th over the six, Zimbabwe needed six runs from the last over, which was bowled by the left-arm spinner Stephen Boock.

Two easy singles reduced the equation to four from four balls. The third was blocked, Butchart heaved at the fourth which hit a pad and bounced out on the offside. John Traicos, the Zimbabwe captain, sprinted down the pitch from the bowlers end, Butchart fell on his back and the run out was a formality. Zimbabwe had made 239.

Houghton made his mark on this form of the game at Trent Bridge in June 1983 when his 84 was one of the principal reasons for Zimbabwe's handsome win over Australia. He is a magnificent driver of the ball, is strong off his pads, and has a lovely square cut as well as quick footwork and a supple wrist, which enables him to improvise.

As was to be expected, New Zealand badly missed Richard Hadlee, Ewan Chatfield bowled well, but Martin Snedden, who had surprisingly

HYDERABAD SCOREBOARD

NEW ZEALAND

M Snedden c Waller b Rawson 64
J Wright c Houghton b Traicos 17
M Crowe c and b Rawson 72
A Jones c Brandes b Ali Shah 0
*J Crowe c Brown b Curran 31
D Patel lbw b Ali Shah 0
J Bracewell not out 13
#I Smith c Brown b Curran 29
S Boock not out 0
Extras (b4, lb5, nb3, w4 16
Total (for 7, 50 overs) 242

Fall of wickets: 1-59, 2-143, 4-166, 5-169, 6-205, 7-240

Did not bat: E. Chatfield, W Watson
Bowling: Curran 10-0-51-2; Rawson 10-0-62-2; Brandes 7-2-23-0; Traicos 10-2-28-1; Butchart 4-0-27-0; Ali Shah 9-0-42-2.

NEW ZEALAND WON BY 3 RUNS

ZIMBABWE

R Brown c J Crowe b Chatfield 1
Ali Shah lbw b Snedden 5
#D Houghton c M Crowe b Snedden 141
A Pycroft run out 12
K Curran c Boock b Watson 4
A Waller c Smith b Watson 5
G Paterson c Smith b Boock 2
P Rawson lbw b Boock 1
I Butchart run out 54
E Brandes run out 0
*J Traicos not out 4
Extras (lb 8, w 1, nb 1) 10
Total (49, 4 overs) 239

Fall of wickets: 1-8, 2-10, 3-61, 4-67, 5-86, 6-94, 7-104, 8-221, 9-221.
Bowling: Chatfield 10-2-26-1; Snedden 9-0-53-2; Bracewell 7-0-47-0; Patel 5-0-27-0; Boock 8, 4-0-42-2.

success as a left-handed opening batsman, and Willie Watson are no more than average county seamers.

Trailcos, the last cricketer on the active list to have played a Test match for South Africa, bowled 10 splendid overs of offbreaks for only 27 runs and checked New Zealand when Martin Crowe threatened to take charge.

DATELINE RAWALPINDI, 13/10/87, MARTIN JOHNSON REPORTS . . .

Lush laments lottery game

It could almost have been England in Rawalpindi yesterday – thick, grey skies, umpires' inspections and, eventually, no play.

The only thing that gave the game away was the persistence of the tannoy announcer, who took the curious view that spectators were entitled to be kept in touch with what was going on. Sunday's electrical storms had done their worst (had it been Bristol the umpires would have been looking again early in the New Year), and so indeed had the World Cup Playing Regulations Committee, who came in for a suitable volley from the England management.

Doubtful though it was that we could have had any cricket at all, the rules do not allow for a start to be made on day one followed by a "carry-over" to day two. Thereby, once past the cut-off point for a game over the minimum distance of 25 overs per side yesterday, it was a case of start again from scratch today.

Of all the full ICC member nations, the TCCB were the lone dissenting voice against this format. The vote was swung by the Australian board, who, as we discovered last winter, are a minor subsidiary of the Channel Nine empire. One-day games that aren't one-day games are hard to market Down Under, and the threat of the Aussies pulling the plug on the TV loot was too great.

The England tour manager Peter Lush, who wanted the match played over the full distance, had several words for yesterday's attempts to cram everything into 25 overs apiece, "farce" and "lottery" among them. He was also critical of the minimum prescription laid down for covering. Only the pitch itself is required to be protected, and while that was fit, the rest of the square was not. There was no shortage of effort to meet the 25-over deadline, but this could not compensate for the shortage of modern technology. The equivalent of our motorised "whale" was an enthusiastic volunteer with a boy's beach bucket, and another was hard at it with a hand-held battery fan.

Elsewhere, the heavy roller was busy ironing an array of blankets, which had clearly provided a five-course meal for the moths. What decided it was a large area of the outfield at the top end. The umpires took the view that the thumbs-up would have been unfair on fine leg, whose location could have been pinpointed only with the aid of a marker buoy and ripples on the surface.

Meanwhile, the sub-continent is already looking to host the 1991 World Cup, and if it boils down to finance, we'll all be here again in four years time. The ICC, palsied body as they are, work like this: everyone makes a "sealed" cash bid except the West Indies (who can barely afford a set of stumps) and India and Pakistan, who are then told who's offering what. They top it, the West Indies automatically vote for the biggest swag, and Bob (or rupee) is your uncle.

A newspaper article yesterday asked: "Why is it ordained that England must have the ICC headquarters come what may? If we can stage the World Cup profitably, we can hold the ICC office as well. Remember, Dunkirk was a retreat!" Well, you can have the ICC with pleasure. Why should Lord's have a monopoly on something as useful as a chocolate teapot when we can ship them all off to Delhi? However, I think they should be told. If the ICC had organised Dunkirk, we'd still be stuck on the beach.

DATELINE RAWALPINDI, 14/10/87, MARTIN JOHNSON REPORTS . . .

PAKISTAN v ENGLAND

Gatting shows England road to batting ruin

Thanks to an hour of unprofessional mayhem, England's challenge for this World Cup now has less in common with the official sponsors, Reliance (as in insurance), than with Reliant (as in three-wheeler). One wheel flew off the wagon in Rawalpindi yesterday.

Victory in their second Group B match would not have guaranteed qualification for the semi-finals, but it would have gone a long way towards it. However, the remarkable way they have managed to defeat the West Indies in Gujranwala last week was not in the same class as the way they contrived to lose to Pakistan here.

There are all sorts of individual awards in this competition, but none for worst stroke. If there was, Mike Gatting's name would be on the cheque. The wretched nature of the England captain's dismissal had such a

Pakistan supporters at Rawalpindi.

debilitating effect that a routine pea-shelling became a collapse that made the Walls of Jericho look like a second-rate conjuring trick.

England, chasing Pakistan's modest 239, needed a further 54 from seven overs with seven wickets in hand when Gatting moved so far outside leg stump to cut a ball from Saleem Jaffer heading for his off-stump that the reason he ultimately missed it was because he was unable to reach it.

In the context of the situation, with Gatting and Allan Lamb quietly milking runs much as they pleased, it was awful, and when England then got themselves into trouble with the asking rate, they panicked so completely that the last six wickets went down for 15 runs in the space of 16 deliveries.

What made it all the more galling was the fact that England failed to make use of winning the toss on a dewy morning, and the absence from Pakistan's attack of their captain, Imran Khan. It was ironic that the first case of the Montezumas to have a bearing on a World Cup game in the sub-continent should have affected one of the host nations. Imran really should not have played when he was unfit, even to toss, and the joust with the coin was conducted between Gatting and Javed Miandad. It was to be the high point of their relationship.

Pakistan had reached 112 for 2 in the 31st over thanks to good batting from Salim Malik, but if Gladstone Small and Derek Pringle had had any luck at all in their opening spells, the game might have been effectively over.

However, Javed, who had entered this game with the phenomenal average of 112 from his previous six one-day innings against England, had come through a sticky start to reach 23 when Phillip DeFreitas formed the opinion that he'd got him out lbw. This was shared by the Australian umpire Tony Crafter, but not by the Pakistan vice-captain. Registering dissent is practised in any number of subtle ways nowadays, but (batting apart) subtlety is not part of Javed's repertoire. He lingered for so long, pointing at a part of his pad several inches higher than the relevant one, that some England players issued him with directions on the shortest route back to the pavilion.

Javed's response was to make two sorties into the assembled throng, and the only thing raised higher than his voice was his bat. Eventually, with the next man in, Ijaz, in danger of being timed out, Javed left – having done nothing to lessen the conviction that one day he will return to the pavilion in the horizontal position.

There were, needless to say, conflicting accounts of the confrontation afterwards. Javed accused Gatting of verbal abuse, and said: "So I told him to shut his mouth." Gatting insisted he did not swear, but when he saw Javed hanging around merely said: "Come on, mate, you're out. For some reason, he then seemed to want to fight about it."

The lastest model of drinks trolley.

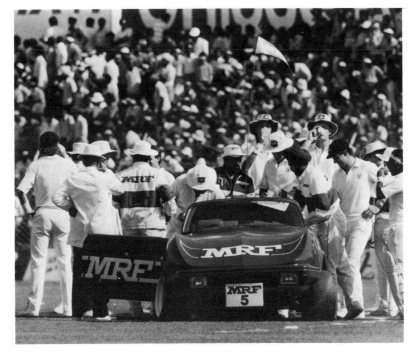

The Pakistani manager, Hasib Ahsan, later attempted to defuse the incident, which must be something of a collector's item. So too was his quote. "Mike Gatting is one of the best gentlemen I know, and the whole thing was just a fly in the ointment."

Gatting did almost get skulled by a flying bat, although it came after normal service had been resumed when Ijaz lost his grip attempting to sweep John Emburey, and the England captain had to take evasive action at square-leg. When Ijaz did connect properly, though, he made a more than useful job of it – and Pakistan eventually set a reasonable total with 50 runs off the final five overs.

Pringle was again the most expensive England bowler, and although Emburey did well in mid-innings, choosing him to bowl the 50th over was not a roaring success. He went for 15 off it, including a six and four to the player destined to decide the match, and be the player of it, Abdul Qadir.

Qadir took four wickets at vital stages, none more so than the first of the innings, that of Graham Gooch, after an opening stand of 52. Gooch

Allan Lamb loses the ball — and his way — as England slide to defeat.

Mike Gatting being interviewed by Tony Lewis after the game.

had looked in prime form, which was certainly not the case with either Chris Broad or Tim Robinson.

Gatting recaptured the initiative but once he'd gone the innings stagnated again, and with 34 required from the last four overs, on came Qadir for his final six deliveries. After the first four of them, England had slumped from 206 for 4 to 207 for 7, with Lamb and Paul Downton both out sweeping, and Emburey run out in between. Pringle and Neil Foster were also run out in photo-finishes, and the game ended when Gladstone Small was leg-before first ball to a full-toss from Jaffer.

RAWALPINDI SCOREBOARD

PAKISTAN

Mansoor Akhtar c Downton b Foster 6
Rameez Raja run out 15
Salim Malik c Downton b DeFreitas 65
Javed Miandad lbw b DeFreitas 23
Ejaz Ahmed c Robinson b Small 59
*Imran Khan b Small 22
Wasim Akram b DeFreitas 5
#Salim Yousuf not out 16
Abdul Qadir not out 12
Extras (lb 10, w 3, nb 3) 16
Total (for 7, 50 overs) 239

Fall of wickets: 1-13, 2-51, 3-112, 4-123, 5-202, 6-210, 7-210.

Did not bat: Tauseef Ahmed, Saleem Jaffer.

Bowling: DeFreitas 10-1-42-3; Foster 10-1-35-1; Small 10-1-47-2; Pringle 10-0-54-0; Emburey 10-0-51-0.

ENGLAND

G A Gooch b Qadir 21
B C Broad b Tauseef 36
R T Robinson b Qadir 33
*M W Gatting b Jaffer 43
A J Lamb lbw b Qadir 30
D R Pringle run out 8
J E Emburey run out 1
#P R Downton c Yousuf b Qadir 0
P A J DeFreitas not out 3
N A Foster run out 6
G C Small lbw b Jaffer 0
Extras (b 6, lb 26, w 8) 40
Total (48.4 overs) 221

Fall of wickets: 1-52, 2-92, 3-141, 4-186, 5-206, 6-207, 7-207, 8-213, 9-221.

Bowling: Akram 9-0-32-0; Jaffer 9.4-0-42-2; Tauseef 10-0-39-1; Qadir 10-0-31-4; Mailk 7-0-29-0; Akhtar 3-0-16-0.

PAKISTAN WON BY 18 RUNS

So this morning, instead of beginning in total control of their group, England (with the West Indies posting a record one-day international total against Sri Lanka to inflate their run-rate) find themselves in third place.

DATELINE MADRAS, 14/10/87, HENRY BLOFELD REPORTS . . .

AUSTRALIA v ZIMBABWE
Australia get retaliation in first

Zimbabwe were unable to do it again. They bowled as well as they can have been expected, restricting Australia to 235 for 7 after putting them in, but when they batted they failed to get anywhere near the run-rate and were all out in 42.4 overs for 139, leaving Australia victors by 96 runs.

Although Zimbabwe are the minnows in the group, there was a professional competence about Australia in the field which was obviously enhanced by the confidence they derived from beating India by one run. They have now won both of their games and look as if they will take some beating.

It is interesting that of the seven games so far, six have been won by the side batting first. In the last year or two the tendency has been for the side winning the toss to field first. This is no longer happening, although Kapil Dev apparently feels it is the only way to win a one-day match.

Australia made a bad start on a pitch which had been used for last Friday's match here. It was even slower yesterday, with a less reliable bounce. Zimbabwe's big chance came in the 10th over, when Allan Border, on 1, did little more than push a ball from Malcolm Jarvis back to the bowler. The left-armer was so surprised that he snatched at it and missed an easy catch.

If that had stuck Australia would have been 21 for 3, with their last pair of specialist batsmen at the crease. As it was, the Zimbabweans made the double mistake of bowling at the legs of Border, who during his innings became the fourth batsman ever to score 4,000 runs in one-day internationals, and over-pitching to Geoff Marsh. These two added 113 in 25 overs before Border holed out to long-on, and although two more wickets fell quickly Steve Waugh and Greg Dyer took Australia well past 200.

Zimbabwe began their innings as if their only plan was not to lose wickets early. They did not, but after nine overs had scored only 13 and never approached the required rate. They could make nothing of Bruce Reid or Craig McDermott and then of course wickets began to fall.

MADRAS SCOREBOARD

AUSTRALIA		ZIMBABWE	
G R Marsh c Curran b Shah	62	R D Brown b O'Donnell	3
D C Boon c Houghton b Curran	2	G A Paterson run out	16
D M Jones run out	2	#D L Houghton c O'Donnell b May	11
*A R Border c Shah b Butchart	67	A J Pycroft run out	9
S R Waugh run out	45	K M Curran b O'Donnell	30
S P O'Donnell run out	3	A C Waller c and b May	19
#G C Dyer c Patterson b Butchart	27	A H Shah b McDermott	2
P L Taylor not out	17	P W E Rawson b Reid	15
C J McDermott c Brown b Curran	1	I P Butchart c Jones b O'Donnell	18
T B A May run out	1	*A J Traicos c and b O'Donnell	6
Extras (w 8)	8	M P Jarvis not out	1
Total (for 9, 50 overs)	235	Extras (b 2, lb 3, w 3, nb 1)	9
		Total (42.4 overs)	139

Fall of wicket: 1-10, 2-20, 3-133, 4-143, 5-154, 6-202, 7-228, 8-230, 9-235.
Did not bat: B A Reid
Bowling: Curran 8-0-29-2; Jarvis 10-0-40-0; Rawson 6-0-39-0; Butchart 10-1-59-2; Traicos 10-0-36-0; Shah 6-0-32-1.

Fall of wicket: 1-20, 2-27, 3-41, 4-44, 5-79, 6-97, 7-97, 8-124, 9-137.
Bowling: McDermott 7-1-13-1; Reid 7-1-21-1; O'Donnell 9.4-1-39-4; Waugh 6-3-7-0; May 8-0-29-2; Taylor 5-0-25-0.

AUSTRALIA WON BY 96 RUNS

David Houghton, the hero against New Zealand, skied Tim May to long-off and only Kevin Curran made any impression with three huge sixes.

DATELINE 14 /10 /87, FROM OUR CORRESPONDENT . . .

SRI LANKA v WEST INDIES
Viv the master goes on run riot

Records tumbled as West Indies' confidence, undermined at the last gasp by England last Friday, soared in the 191-run thrashing they administered to the hapless Sri Lankans in Karachi.

After scoring only 27 against England, it was predictable that Viv Richards would hold centrestage, particularly against a bowling attack as friendly as Sri Lanka's. His 181 – beating Kapil Dev's 175 against Zimbabwe in 1983 – was the highest in World Cup history, and his side's total of 360 for 4 was a record for any one-day international, whether of 50 or 60 overs per side.

Richards, who went in on a hat-trick after Ravi Ratnayake had dismissed Carlisle Best and Richie Richardson, was in for only 125 deliveries, stroking six sixes and 16 fours. He took a sedate 62 balls to reach his half-century, 35 more to reach his 10th one-day international century, and only 15 to get to 150. His last 81 runs came off 33 deliveries.

Amid the welter of Richards' statistics, Desmond Haynes' century was overshadowed. Haynes, only one international one-day hundred behind Richards, made 105, and shared a third-wicket stand of 182 runs in 177 balls with his captain. The masterly Richards was especially severe on Ratnayake, punishing his presumption in removing Best and Richardson by taking 44 off two overs – 22 more than the medium-pacer had conceded in his first five overs put together,

But the worst-affected of the shell-shocked Sri Lankan bowlers was another medium-pacer, Asantha de Mel, whose 10 overs cost 97, not quite enough to take the World Cup's worst-figures record, which is still held by New Zealand's Martin Snedden.

After such merciless punishment in the field, it was no surprise that the Sri Lankan batting was unable to maintain anything like the rapid progress – 7.2 runs an over – they needed, although 16 came off Patrick Patterson's first over and eight off Courtney Walsh's first two deliveries.

Walsh's third accounted for Roshan Mahanama, and once Sri Lanka slipped to 57 for 3 all hope was gone. They lost only one further wicket and ended on 169 for 4, but Richards preferred to save his front-line bowlers, once his victory was settled, for the more important attack on the Pakistanis in Lahore on Friday.

KARACHI SCOREBOARD

WEST INDIES

D L Haynes b Gurusingha 105
C A Best b Ratnayake 18
R B Richardson c Kuruppu b Ratnayake 0
/I V A Richards c Mahanama b De Mel 181
A L Logie not out 31
R A Harper not out 5
Extras (b 4, lb 8, nb 4, w 4) 20
Total (for 4, 50 overs) 360

Fall of wickets: 1-45, 2-45, 3-227, 4-343.
Did not bat: C L Hooper, #P J Dujon, W K M Benjamin, C A Walsh, B P Patterson.
Bowling: John 10-1-48-0, J R Ratnayake 8-0-68-2; Anurasiri 10-0-39-0, De Mel 10-0-97-1; De Silva 6-0-35-0; Ranatunga 2-0-18-0; Gurusingha 4-0-43-1.

WEST INDIES WON BY 191 RUNS

SRI LANKA

R Mahanama c Dujon b Walsh 12
#B Kuruppu lbw b Patterson 14
A Gurusingha b Hooper 36
P de Silva c Dujon b Hooper 9
A Ranatunga not out 52
*D Mendis not out 37
Extras (b 1, lb 2, w 6) 9
Total (for 4, 50 overs) 169

Fall of wickets: 1-24, 2-31, 3-57, 4-112.
Did not bat: R Madugalle, J R Ratnayake, A de Mel, V John, S. Anurasiri.
Bowling: Patterson 7-0-32-1; Walsh 7-2-23-1; Harper 10-2-15-0; Benjamin 4-0-11-0; Hooper 10-0-39-2; Richards 8-0-22-0; Richardson 4-0-24-0.

DATELINE PESHAWAR, 15/10/87, MARTIN JOHNSON REPORTS...

Pringle's firing line

As England flew out to Khyber Pass country today to prepare for Saturday's Group B match against Sri Lanka in Peshawar, they took with them the reputation of being, if not the best, at least the most versatile team in this World Cup. As yet, no one else has managed to win when it was impossible not to lose, and lose when it was impossible not to win.

Had it not been for Tuesday's 18-run defeat by Pakistan, Australia and England would currently be top of their respective groups – not at all what the organisers had in mind. Now, there is precious little margin for error, and not even four wins out of six can guarantee qualification for the semi-finals.

At the players' request, England held a lengthy inquest into what went wrong in Rawalpindi, and manager Micky Stewart said: "I personally thought we shouldn't have paced our innings to leave as much as six and a half an over to get off the last 10. This was not a unanimous view, however, and with seven wickets in hand we really should have got the runs anyway."

On the evidence of the two games played so far, England's best plan would appear to be to orchestrate a position of needing something like 10 an over from the final 10, with Allan Lamb and Neil Foster at the crease. It would seem, though, that against Pakistan they paid the penalty for lack of foresight over selection – not just on Tuesday morning, but also before leaving home.

In the enforced absence of David Gower and Ian Botham, there are deficiencies in batsmen who can both score quick runs and also save them in the field. Lancashire's Neil Fairbrother would have improved both departments, and what wouldn't we have given to have seen either Peter Willey or David Capel coming in at No. 6 on Tuesday?

England were also, as we suspected, not brave enough to change a winning team. The euphoria surrounding the West Indies game should not have been allowed to disguise one or two clear warning signals from Gujranwala.

Unless a wicket falls quickly, Mike Gatting will have to be prepared to move up to No. 3, and the fielding is far too suspect for Bill Athey to be employed any longer as one of the dressing-room attendants. It is also difficult to see how Derek Pringle can be persevered with in his current form. He is struggling for both line and length with his bowling, and his bat might just as well have been left at Heathrow's excess baggage counter.

On the morning after the Rawalpindi match, Ray Illingworth remarked over breakfast that Keith Fletcher had made the confident pre-tour forecast that Pringle would be a "banker with both bat and ball". This was quickly followed by a comment from the next table: "Are you sure he said banker?"

However, it is difficult not to feel for the ever-affable Pringle, who might well have rediscovered his confidence on Tuesday given a reasonable slice of good fortune. His third delivery was edged for four, his fifth resulted in a dropped catch by Chris Broad, and Javed Miandad survived an early lbw appeal against him that looked an even better shout than Phillip DeFreitas's successful one later on.

If there was any consolation to come out of the match, it was probably the fact that Abdul Qadir was the man of it. The next wildlife series to deal with endangered species really ought to include the leg-spinner, and for Qadir to be playing such a major influence in this type of cricket is warming news for those with broader long-term interests than England's immediate well-being.

The World Cup is certainly creating massive interest in the sub-continent, although going down a bomb would perhaps be an inappropriate phase. Internal politics are so volatile that a day does not pass without news of someone being blown up somewhere – and England's next stop, Peshawar, does not conjure up visions of cream teas and Canterbury.

Two days ago a bus shelter was ripped apart with 13 casualties, and yesterday someone lobbed a kilo of gelignite into Peshawar's Iranian Culture Centre. Most disturbing of all, the match itself has already been the subject of three separate bomb threats.

Peshawar, though, is small beer in the TNT league compared to England's fourth World Cup venue, Karachi, where every night appears to be Guy Fawkes Night. Bomb threats in England are fortunately still rare enough to prompt evacuations, but so many bits of Karachi are rearranged daily that panic is an understandably natural reaction. A hoax call to a school yesterday morning left a dozen children seriously injured in a stampede to get out.

None of this has so far touched the cricket, and the security arrangements could hardly be more thorough. However, the mere fact that every adult male here appears to be wearing a uniform and carrying a machine gun, is evidence enough that protection is required on a worrying scale.

DATELINE BANGALORE, 15/10/87, HENRY BLOFELD REPORTS . . .

INDIA v NEW ZEALAND
India recover composure

The cricket was disappointingly patchy in a game which had promised so much and in the end India won rather more convincingly than a 16-run margin of victory suggests. After being sent in, India recovered from a poor start and finished with 252 for 7.

When their turn came, New Zealand were given a good start by Martin Snedden and Ken Rutherford – John Wright had 'flu – but when Martin Crowe failed they did not have anyone else of the same calibre who might have made a match of it. New Zealand finished at 236 for 8 which gave India an important victory and the likelihood must be that India and Australia will go through to the semi-finals from this group.

The game was only eight overs old before two outrageous pieces of running by Kris Srikkanth had cost Sunil Gavaskar and himself their wickets. When, with the score 23, Dilip Vengsakar checked a drive and gave Willy Watson a return catch the 50,000 crowd was almost eerily silent.

A temporary palliative for India was provided by Navjot Siddhu, who looks a more impressive batsman each time he goes to the crease. But then Sidhu, Mohammad Azharudin and Ravi Shastri all got themselves out when there was no need.

At 170 for 7 in the 42nd over, India looked likely to be short of runs but that did not allow for Kapil Dev who, with Kiran More, put on 82 runs off the last 45 balls.

BANGALORE SCOREBOARD

INDIA

K. Srikkanth run out	9
S Gavaskar run out	2
N Sidhu c Jones b Patel	75
D Vengasarkar c and b Watson	0
M Azharuddin c Boock b Patel	21
R Shastri c and b Patel	22
*Kapil Dev not out	72
M Prabhakar c and b Chatfield	3
#K More not out	42
Extras (lb 4, w 2)	6
Total (for 7, 50 overs)	**252**

Fall of wickets: 1-11, 2-16, 3-21, 4-86, 5-114, 6-165, 7-170.
Did not bat: Maninder Singh, L Shavaramakrishnan.
Bowling: Chatfield 10-1-39-1; Snedden 10-1-56-0; Watson 9-0-59-1; Boock 4-0-26-0; Bracewell 7-0-32-0; Patel 10-0-36-3.

INDIA WON BY 16 RUNS

NEW ZEALAND

M Snedden c Shastri b Azharuddin	33
K Rutherford c Srikkanth b Shastri	75
M Crowe st More b Maninder	9
A Jones run out	64
*J Crowe c Vengsarkar b Maninder	7
D Patel run out	1
J Bracewell c Maninder b Shastri	8
#I Smith b Prabhakar	10
S Boock not out	7
W Watson not out	2
Extras (lb 9, b 5, nb 1, w 5)	20
Total (for 8, 50 overs)	**236**

Fall of wickets: 1-67, 2-86, 3-146, 4-168, 5-170, 6-189, 7-206, 8-225.
Did not bat: E Chatfield.
Bowling: Kapil Dev 10-1-54-0; Prabhakar 8-0-38-1; Azharuddin 4-0-11-1; Shavaramakrishnan 8-0-34-0; Maninider 10-0-40-2; Shastri 10-0-45-2.

DATELINE PESHAWAR, 16/10/87, MARTIN JOHNSON REPORTS...

Stewart rules Gatting out of order

England arrived in the troubled North-west Frontier town of Peshawar last night with the accent heavily on security – but, for all the troops and rifles keeping them company, the only loud bang thus far came on Tuesday when they shot themselves in the foot. A sightseeing trip to the border is not recommended, but if England lose to Sri Lanka tommorrow they will be well and truly up the Khyber.

As far as the position in Group B is concerned, today's match between Pakistan and the West Indies in Lahore is of almost equal importance. If the West Indies win, and presuming England do otherwise, three teams will be level at eight points apiece – which would maintain the possibility of someone winning four games out of six and still going out on scoring rates.

Mike Gatting and Micky Stewart have differing views on whom they would like to win in Lahore, as indeed they do on the captain's position in the batting order. For what it is worth, I would make it 2-0 to the manager.

Gatting says he would like to go into the second half of the group fixtures all square with Pakistan and the West Indies, but Stewart would prefer to see a Pakistani win today and the West Indies cast temporarily adrift in third place. He also wants to see Gatting up the order at No. 3, and, as far as that is concerned, he may get his wish tomorrow.

England have a fitness doubt about Neil Foster, who has an inflamed left knee and is rated as no better than 50-50. This would appear to increase the prospects of Derek Pringle retaining his place, which might leave one or two of you at home inflamed as well. However, even if Foster does make it, Pringle is still under threat from either Paul Jarvis or Eddie Hemmings, and the Nottinghamshire spinner may have emerged as slight favourite given that the pitch is quite unlike some of the more shadily cultivated fields around here, in that it has no grass.

Stewart appears to have talked Gatting around into batting at three ("unless we lose an early wicket I feel that's where he should always bat"), despite the captain's opinion that he is better off lower down in case of emergencies.

A former Charlton Athletic and Corinthian Casuals inside-forward, Stewart is fond of football analogies. He said: "If we get a decent start we want to cash in. The sooner you go 3-0 up the better."

If Pringle does play, and the vibes suggest that he will, he may swap places in the order with Paul Downton, who is a much better improviser in this type of cricket. There is also, Stewart admitted, some consideration being given to picking Bill Athey to perk up fielding that fluctuates between the ordinary and geriatric.

One thing is certain. If England do not bowl well, their opponents will score a lot of runs. The Sri Lankans can't bowl to save their lives, but their batsmen give it a fearful wallop offered half a chance, and almost caused an upset in the opening World Cup game against the Pakistanis. It is also pertinent to recall that England do not have a 100 per cent record against Sri Lanka in four previous one-day internationals, having lost by three runs in Colombo in 1982.

England seem likely to stick by their policy of batting second if they win the toss, despite the fact that their victory over the West Indies in Gujranwala was the only occasion in eight games so far that the team going in first had lost.

PAKISTAN v WEST INDIES
Pakistan fired by the rupee motive

If there was cause for a mild shout of "whoopee" from the England camp at the news of the West Indies' second Group B defeat in Lahore yesterday, the chorus from the Pakistan dressing-room would undoubtably have been "rupee". This World Cup may be all about glory, but where the host nations are concerned, glory actually does pay the bills.

Pakistan's gripping victory, off the final delivery and with the last pair at the crease, ought to guarantee England outright second place in their group after today's game against Sri Lanka in Peshawar.

One suspected before the competition began that if England were to qualify for the semi-finals, it might have to be at the expense of the West Indies rather than Pakistan, and that is how it is turning out. It was also thought before leaving home that England's major disadvantage here would be climate and crowd hostility. This may still be true, but only perhaps by a shade from the fact that the two host-country teams are being motivated by what appears to turn them on best of all – cash.

India's cricket board secretary N K P Salve made this discovery after the 1979 final when, according to his recently-published book (which,

Pakistan fans queue to watch the Lahore match.

incidentally, makes *Thommo* read like a work of literary genius), the first question put to him by Kapil Dev and Sunil Gavaskar in the Lord's dressing room was "how much?"

Salve then claimed that they got him drunk on champagne, and wheedled so many public promises of extra rupees out of him that he had to go on a rounding-up-of-sponsors mission to avoid having to cough up himself.

After Pakistan's win over England on Tuesday, however, sponsors were trampling each other to death in the rush. General Zia was first to set the ball rolling with an instant cheque for 100,000 rupees (£25,000), a textile company shelled out another £8,000 between six players, and a clothing manufacturer chipped in with cash awards for fours, sixes and catches.

Yesterday's victory may make all this look nothing more than a cursory dip into the petty-cash box, and Pakistan go on to win the competition, there is gold on the way from a firm called "Touchme", the official cosmetics supplier to the World Cup. There is an "official" supplier for everything in the World Cup, as it happens, from teabags and ice cream to paper hankies.

Badly in need of another box of official tissues is the West Indies fast bowler Courtney Walsh, who burst into tears after England got the 13 they needed from his final over in Gujranwala. Against Pakistan he had 14 to play with, and blew it again.

The West Indies, the only team batting first to lose a game until yesterday, made only 216 after winning the toss, but looked like defending it successfully with 12 overs to go. Pakistan had just lost their fifth wicket, Javed's, and were faced with an asking rate of seven runs an over when Salim Yousuf – he of the Barnes Wallis catches – knocked a hole in the old adage that cheats never prosper. While he was still adjusting his sights, the West Indies dropped him three times off successive balls from Eldine Baptiste.

Yousuf might just make a half-decent long-stop if someone issued him with a horse blanket, but he can't half bat, and once the nerves had settled he smashed his team back into the match with a rapid half-century.

The crowd enjoyed it more than those watching on television, which went on the blink for 20 crucial minutes, and they had to make do with sound only during the Urdu commentary shift. I have to say that the English version here is only marginally more comprehensible. The picture was back just in time for Yousuf's dismissal, and when Walsh bowled the fateful final over. Abdul Qadir had Pakistan's only thoroughbred rabbit, Saleem Jaffer, to keep him company.

Walsh also had it in his power to win the game off the final ball, but may have decided that his life was more valuable than a World Cup

Saleem Jaffer scurries home safely as Courtney Walsh is about to receive the ball.

winner's medal. Qadir, having just smashed a six over lone-off, needed a single to win it (on the fewer-wickets-lost rule) when Walsh ran in to bowl the final ball. Jaffer, though, was so fast out of the blocks that Walsh, startled to find himself bowling to two batsmen, stopped in his delivery stride. He could have run out Jaffer by half a pitch-length, but opted for the warning (and a non-lynching) instead, and was then sliced away for the winning two by an ecstatic Qadir.

If security was less than water-tight in Lahore – Qadir was engulfed by what appeared to be half of Pakistan before being chaired off – England continued to be well chaperoned by the armed forces in not very peaceful Peshawar yesterday, both during morning practise, and a spot of post-prandial golf.

If there is a worry, it is that everyone is so friendly, including the police and army. Three years ago in Bombay, shortly after the Percy Norris shooting, an England press photographer, dressed in what looked like a combat jacket and carrying two large cloth-covered lenses, decided to test security.

"Excuse me" he asked the highest-ranking officer he could find. "I'm from the IRA. Could you direct me to the England dressing-room?" He was immediately given a VIP escort, and before you could say Tim Robinson he was shaking hands with, er, Tim Robinson. As it happens.

Abdul Qadir and Hasib Ahsan are escorted from the field after a famous victory.

LAHORE SCOREBOARD

WEST INDIES

D Haynes b Jaffer 37
P Simmons c and b Tauseef 50
R Richardson c Ejaz b Jaffer 11
* I V A Richards c Malik b Imran 51
G Logie c Akhtar b Jaffer 2
C Hooper lbw b Akram 22
#J Dujon lbw b Akram 5
R Harper c Mansoor b Imran 0
E Baptiste b Imran 14
C Walsh lbw b Imran 7
P Patterson not out 0
Extras (b 1, lb 14, w 2) 17
Total (49.3 overs) **216**

Fall of wickets: 1-91, 2-97, 3-118, 4-121, 5-169,
6-184, 7-184, 8-196, 9-207.
Bowling: Imran 8.3-2-37-4; Akram 10-0-45-2;
Qadir 8-0-42-0; Tauseef 10-2-35-1; Jaffer
10-0-30-3; Malik 3-0-12-0.

PAKISTAN WON BY 1 RUN

PAKISTAN

Rameez Raja c Richards b Harper 42
Mansoor Akhtar b Patterson 10
Saleem Malik c Baptiste b Walsh 4
Javed Miandad c and b Hooper 33
Ejaz Ahmed b Walsh 6
*Imran Khan c Logie b Walsh 18
#Salim Yousuf c Hooper b Walsh 56
Wasim Akram c Richardson b Patterson 7
Abdul Qadir not out 16
Tauseef Ahmad run out 0
Saleem Jaffer not out 1
Extras (b 5, lb 12, w 7) 24
Total (for 9, 50 overs) **217**

Fall of wickets: 1-23, 2-28, 3-92, 4-104, 5-110,
6-183, 7-200, 8-202, 9-203.
Bowling: Patterson 10-1-51-2; Walsh
10-1-40-4; Baptiste 8-1-33-0; Harper 10-0-28-1;
Hooper 10-0-38-1; Richards 2-0-10-0.

ENGLAND v SRI LANKA
Golden year ends for Broad

Sorrow was not the operative word when England packed their bags in Peshawar yesterday. The players were as happy to get out without being bombed as they were with four more World Cup points, the Press discovered the ideal location for "Carry On Up The Telephone Exchange", and it's a fair bet that the locals weren't too distressed either.

The inhabitants of this impoverished North-west Frontier city can rarely wake up of a morning expecting any light relief from a humdrum existence – and those who did on Saturday, because the World Cup was in town, were sadly disappointed. England were far too efficient for Sri Lanka and, on lop-sided occasions like these, very little can rival a one-day cricket match for tedium.

It should all be very different in Karachi tomorrow, when England meet a team who are not only extremely difficult to beat, but against whom the very thought of winning – as we saw in Rawalpindi – can persuade us to beat ourselves.

Victory over Pakistan, who have won all three of their games, would mean that England could get away with losing their fifth group match, to the West Indies in Jaipur, and still qualify by beating Sri Lanka again in the sixth and last at Pune.

What also seems probable is that Chris Broad, who has not looked in good form, will be dropped for the first time since embarking on the golden run in Australia last winter that earned him the international cricketer-of-the-year award. The greater fluency of Tim Robinson and Bill Athey against spin on a Karachi pitch that usually turns may prompt England to select them both for the first time so far.

It also follows that Eddie Hemmings will remain, and Neil Foster, now recovered from his knee injury, is certain to return. Less certain is for whom? It really ought to be Derek Pringle, but the selectors may leave out Gladstone Small instead.

Mike Gatting, who put both the West Indies and Pakistan in before having a chage of heart in Peshawar, may also bat first again in Karachi if his luck with the toss holds. So far the pitches have tended to lose what little early pace they do have, making strokeplay more difficult.

The one used in Peshawar certainly got slower, while at lunchtime – with England dining happily on a total of 296 – something horribly similar to a bomb reverberated around the stadium.

Graham Gooch batting against Sri Lanka.

Actually, it was thunder, and although Sri Lanka's reply got off to a prompt start, there was a constant threat of more rain. England, therefore, were in a great hurry to complete the minimum 25 overs that would constitute a result.

Five overs were eventually lost to the weather, but by then, the Sri Lankan innings was more than halfway through, and they finished 109 runs short of their target of 267 from 40 overs.

Confirmation of the suspicion that their bowlers are not up to the task came when Graham Gooch made an effortless 84 from 100 balls and Allan Lamb smashed a couple of sixes in his 76 from 58, while Gatting's elevation to No. 3 provided the injection of top-order urgency that had hitherto been missing. Lamb and John Emburey put on 69 together in five overs, and England's total provided useful insurance (as provided by the World Cup sponsors) in a group that might yet revolve around scoring rates.

PERSHAWAR SCOREBOARD

ENGLAND

G A Gooch c and b Anurasiri 84
B C Broad c DeSilva b J R Ratnayake 28
*M W Gatting b R J Ratnayake 58
A J Lamb c DeSilva b J R Ratnayake 76
J E Emburey not out 30
C W J Athey not out 2
Extras (lb 13, w 5) 18
Total (for 4, 50 overs) 296

Fall of wickets: 1-89, 2-142, 3-218, 4-287.
Did not bat: D R Pringle, #P R Downton, P A J DeFreitas, E E Hemmings, G C Small.
Bowling: J R Ratnayake 9-0-62-2-; John 10-0-44-0; DeSilva 7-0-33-0; R J Ratnayake 10-0-61-1; Anurasiri 8-0-44-1; Ranatunga 6-0-40-0.

Umpires: V Ramaswamy and R Gupta (India).

ENGLAND WON BY 138 RUNS

SRI LANKA

R S Manahanama c Gooch b Pringle 11
#D S B Kuruppu c Hemmings b Emburey 13
A P Gurusinha run out 1
R S Madugalle b Hemmings 30
A Ranatunga lbw b DeFreitas 40
*L R D Mendis run out 14
P A DeSilva c Emburey b Hemmings 6
J R Ratnayake c Broad b Emburey 1
R J Ratnayake not out 14
V B John not out 8
Extras (b 2, lb 9, w 6, nb 3) 20
Total (for 8, 45 overs) 158

Fall of wicket: 1-31; 2-32, 3-37, 4-99, 5-105, 6-113, 7-119, 8-137.
Did not bat: S D Arunasiri.
Bowling: DeFreitas 9-2-24-1; Small 7-0-27-0; Pringle 4-1-11-1; Emburey 10-1-26-2; Hemmings 10-1-31-2; Gooch 2-0-9-0; Athey 1-0-10-0; Broad 1-0-6-0; Lamb 1-0-3-0.

John Emburey takes a well-earned rest.

INDIA v ZIMBABWE

Zimbabwe's World Cup interest was virtually ended when India trounced them by eight wickets with 22 overs to spare in Saturday's Group A match in Bombay.

BOMBAY SCOREBOARD

ZIMBABWE

G A Paterson b Prabhaker	6
K Arnott lbw b Prabhakar	1
†D L Houghton b Prabhakar	0
A J Pycroft st More b Shastri	61
K M Curran c More b Prabhakar	0
A C Waller st More b Maninder	16
I P Butchart c Shivaramakrishnan b Maninder	10
A H Shah c More b Maninder	0
M A Meman run out	19
*A J Traicos c Gavaskar b Shivaramakrishnan	0
M P Jarvis not out	8
Extras (b 2, lb 6, w 6)	14
Total (44.2 overs)	135

Fall of wickets: 1-3, 2-12, 3-13, 4-13, 5-47, 6-67, 7-67, 8-98, 9-99.
Bowling: Kapil Dev 8-1-17-0; Prabhakar 8-1-19-4; Maninder 10-0-21-3; Azharuddin 1-0-6-0; Shivaramakrishnan 9-0-36-1; Shastri 8.2-0-28-1.

INDIA

K Srikkanth c Paterson b Traicos	31
S M Gavaskar st Houghton b Traicos	43
M Prabhakar not out	11
D B Vengsarkar not out	46
Extras (w 4, lb 1)	5
Total (2 wkts, 27.5 overs)	136

Fall of wickets: 1-76, 2-80.
Did not bat: N S Sidhu, M Azharuddin, *Kapil Dev, R J Shastri, †K S More, L Shivaramakrishnan, Maninder Singh.
Bowling: Curran 6-0-32-0; Jarvis 4-0-22-0; Butchart 3-0-20-0; Traicos 8-0-27-2, Meman 6.5-0-34-0.
Man of the match: M Prabhakar.

INDIA WON BY 8 WICKETS

AUSTRALIA v NEW ZEALAND

Australia - another narrow win

After an heroic effort to make 200 to beat Australia in a truncated 30-over match at the Nehru Stadium, New Zealand threw it all away in the last over when they needed seven to win with four wickets in hand. Australia, who won by three runs, are now virtually assured of a semi-final place.

Heavy rain on Sunday evening prevented a start until soon after midday, and the outfield and the bowlers' run-ups were still very wet and slippery. Australia were put in, and were taken to 199 largely as a result of a spirited innings of 87 by David Boon.

New Zealand were then given an excellent start by John Wright, who has recovered from a nasty attack of 'flu, and Ken Rutherford. They put on 83 in 13 overs for the first wicket, and after they had gone Martin Crowe played a delightful innings of 58 which looked for a time as if it would be decisive.

New Zealand needed 59 from five overs. The two bowled by Craig McDermott produced 16, and in the end Steve Waugh bowled the last over with seven still wanted. In Madras in the first Group A match, he had also bowled the last over, and with his sixth ball knocked out Maninder Singh's off-stump for Australia to win that game by one run.

This time Waugh bowled his first ball to Martin Crowe, who seemed to panic. He drove wildly and skied it to deep extra-cover, where Geoff Marsh held a good running catch. Ian Smith faced the next ball, which pitched in the block hole and yorked him.

A single was scampered off the third by Willie Watson, and Martin Snedden took another single off the fourth. Watson then pushed the fifth back to the bowler. Waugh fielded quickly and ran out Snedden, who had started for a run.

With five needed to win, the last ball produced a single and New Zealand were to all intents and purposes out of the competition, knowing that they had only themselves to blame for panicking at the end. But without Richard Hadlee they have never really looked as if they were going to win out of their group and into the last four.

At the start, Australia soon lost Marsh, caught at first slip trying to run Snedden down to third man, but then Boon and Dean Jones produced a stirring partnership of 120 in 17 overs.

They profited mainly against the off-spin of John Bracewell and Dipak Patel who obviously had difficulty in holding a ball which must have been like a cake of soap. They reached a 100 stand in only 63 balls.

After Jones had been well caught by Rutherford juggling at long-on from a full toss by Patel, Allan Border enlivened the final overs. It was grand entertainment and another medal for Australia who are not going to be that easy to beat.

INDORE SCOREBOARD

AUSTRALIA

D C Boon c Wright b Snedden	87
G R Marsh c J Crowe b Snedden	5
D M Jones c Rutherford b Patel	52
*A R Border c M Crowe b Chatfield	34
S R Waugh not out	13
T W Moody not out	0
Extras (b 1, lb 5, w 2)	8
Total (for 4, 30 overs)	**199**

Fall of wickets: 1-17, 2-134, 3-171, 4-196.
Did not bat: S P O'Donnell, #G C Dyer, C J McDermott. T B A May, B A Reid.
Bowling: Snedden 6-0-35-2; Chatfield 6-0-28-1; Watson 6-0-34-0; Patel 6-0-45-1; Braccewell 6-0-51-1.

Umpires: D Archer (West Indies) and K Hyat (Pakistan).

AUSTRALIA WON BY 3 RUNS

NEW ZEALAND

K Rutherford b O'Donnell	37
J Wright c Dyer b O'Donnell	47
M Crowe c Marsh b Waugh	58
A Jones c Marsh b McDermott	15
#J Crowe c and b Reid	3
D Patel run out	13
J Bracewell c and b Reid	6
#I Smith b Waugh	1
M Snedden run out	1
E Chatfield not out	0
W Watson not out	2
Extras (b 4, lb 5, w 4)	13
Total (for 9, 30 overs)	**196**

Fall of wickets: 1-83, 2-94, 3-133, 4-140, 5-165, 6-183, 7-193, 8-193, 9-195.
Bowling: McDermott 6-0-30-1; Reid 6-0-38-3; May 6-0-39-0; O'Donnell 6-0-44-2; Waugh 6-0-36-2.

DATELINE KARACHI, 20/10/87, MARTIN JOHNSON REPORTS...

Downton's cheek feels the force

If England thought they were well protected during practise for today's important Group B match against Pakistan in the national stadium – after all, it's not every day you take a net after it has been swept for mines – they reckoned without an air attack launched by one of their own players.

Despite the best efforts of the Karachi Bomb Squad yesterday, who combed the 30,000-seater staium with official World Cup mine detectors, Paul Downton still managed to end up in hospital when a cricket ball propelled from Phil DeFreitas's bat 60 or so yards away exploded into his left cheekbone.

The ball was certainly travelling (it would have been a flattish six over long-off on most grounds you can think of) and Downton, who was busy chatting to captain Mike Gatting at the time, was eventually helped away with an ugly swelling having completely closed the left eye.

He was remarkably fortunate that there was no fracture, as indeed were England. With only 14 men per squad, and all the other ways of losing players on the sub-continent (Paul Jarvis had already been ruled out because of illness) you need freak training accidents out here like you do laxative chewing-gum.

Downton paid the penalty for relaxing over the absence of Ian Botham, whose low boredom threshold prompts him to treat net practise as a form of pigeon shoot. Gatting said ruefully "It could have happened a thousand times for Both but never has."

This was probably unfair on Botham, who has an exceptional aim and is highly selective in his targets – passing pressmen being a particular personal favourite. Downton, the only specialist wicketkeeper in the party, was expected to play today, but the decision was not being made until this morning. Bill Athey, with strictly limited experience behind the strumps, was the likely, but hardly welcome, replacement.

The venue for today's match looks a little but like a miniature Melbourne, although there are hints of Headingley – in that the England players also regard that as a potential minefield – and Trent Bridge. Yesterday, the local version of Ron Allsopp was rolling grass clippings into it too.

Security is extremely tight, as Karachi is not only the centre of Pakistan commerce, but also of the country's amateur bomb enthusiasts, ranging from disaffected students to Afghan communists.

As long as no one tries to blow them up, however, the players are certainly well catered for. If you cleared the armchairs and individual lockers away, England's dressing-room could stage the match in the event of rain.

The Press accommodation is not quite as palatial, but it was a comfort to see a plaque on the wall proclaiming "Fumigon! This premises is absolutely hygenic!" It is hardly necessary to add, and there it was in letters bold and clear – that Fumigon is the official fumigation firm of the World Cup.

Pakistan, meanwhile, went into the match knowing that a second victory over England would not only virtually guarantee qualification for the semi-finals, but also prompt another avalanche of rupees from various benefactors.

After their final-ball win over the West Indies several players received cash bonuses ranging from £2,500 (Imran) to £500, but this was small change compared with Abdul Qadir, who collected £20,000 from two local businessmen alone. Courtney Walsh, incidentally, who has effectively lost the West Indies both their matches, was presented with a carpet for not running out Salim Jaffer off the final ball. He was last seen trying to fly home on it.

DATELINE KARACHI, 21 /10 /87, MARTIN JOHNSON REPORTS . . .

PAKISTAN v ENGLAND

More one-day blunders make England suffer

As everything else in this competition is prefixed by the word "official" we may discover in Jaipur next week whether England can pip the West Indies for the title of official World Cup squanderers of winning positions. On the face of it, the Windies represent formidable opposition, but while they are last-over specialists the evidence suggests that England can sustain their cock-ups over much longer periods.

Finding a way to lose to Pakistan in Rawalpindi was far from easy, but England came pretty close to matching that abysmal effort at the National Stadium yesterday. They certainly pulled it off with more to spare this time, and the Jaipur match now becomes a virtual knock-out to determine who qualifies from Group B with Pakistan.

In a way, yesterday's defeat was more disturbing than Rawalpindi where, apart from the selectors getting the wrong 14 in the first place, it was also apparent that they had then contrived to come up with the wrong 11. Yesterday's side (minus Broad, Jarvis and Pringle) was more like it, so one now suspects that England may simply not be good enough.

The pitch was slowish, but with greater uniformity of bounce than we have seen so far, and England ought to have made around 270-280. What

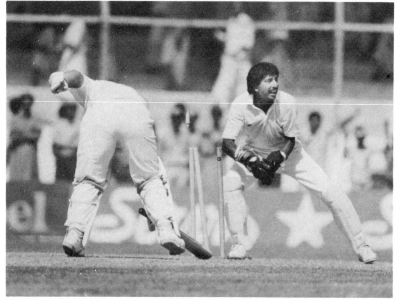

Salim Yousuf attempts to run out Mike Gatting.

they ended up with, 244, sounds okay, but in fact represented a crucial psychological swing to the opposition.

The opposition, as it happened, were in a pretty generous mood. Imran took the curious view that England would not enjoy batting first on a scorching day, and Pakistan's fielding was as patchy as we have seen from any side so far other than, er, England. Our old friend Salim Yousuf set the tone when he dropped Tim Robinson in the opening over, almost an action replay of Botham at Headingley. The one difference this time was that Yousuf didn't appeal after retrieving the ball from the turf.

Yousuf, who has obviously been brushing up on his laws, then missed stumping Mike Gatting, and the England captain also survived a slip chance to the official World Cup pain-in-the-neck Javed Miandad. About half an hour later, the two of them were (shades of Rawalpindi) again involved in a public outbreak of mutual dislike.

During the second drinks interval, Javed, in that uniquely endearing way of his, grabbed the Indian umpire Ramaswamy and complained that Gatting and Bill Athey were deliberately scuffing up the pitch. This was followed by two separate verbal confrontations between Gatting and living legend, as one local newspaper referred to Javed before the match. How long he can remain so (living as opposed to legend) is a matter for conjecture, and stand by for some fun and games in the Test series when he inherits the captaincy from Imran.

If Javed was the only one to put his emotions on display, the entire Pakistan side had good reason to feel tetchy at the time. Gatting and Athey were quietly putting the game beyond their reach with a third-wicket partnership of 135 in 24 overs – greatly assisted by Imran's incomprehensibile use of Salim Malik as a sixth bowler. Malik is on the slow side of medium, does not spin, seam it or swing it, and yet by using him Imran and Wasim Akram gave up three overs between them.

Athey played beautifully right from the start, but Gatting's half-century was no less meritorious in that (in more ways than one) he did not look at all his normal self. The glass in the press-box window gave everyone a funfair house-of-mirrors appearance and had the unique effect of making Gatting look 7ft tall and wafer-thin. Rather like a bearded Agnew, in fact. He does, though, have the priceless knack of keeping his score ticking over when he is out of touch.

The turning point came at 187 for 2 from 37 overs when Athey – whose 102-ball innings had included two majestic sixes – and Gatting went in the space of three deliveries. Athey, as far as we know, has never before played the reverse sweep for England, and one hopes he never will again. He got his legs into a sort of position that is normally not possible when you are sober, and he was bowled by Tauseef.

With two new batsmen in, England never regained their momentum, and the gamble taken by picking Pringle for the World Cup was acutely shown up by the sight of Emburey coming in at No. 6. An eccentric hitter he may be – it's a toss-up as to who is more baffled by whom when he is facing Qadir – but at this level, nothing more than that. In their final 13 overs, England lost seven wickets for 57, and any hopes they might still have entertained of defending 244 were quashed by catching Pakistan's complaint of non-catching. Ramiz Raja, well though he played for his maiden one-day international century, was dropped twice – the first, when only six – an absurdly easy chance to Gatting at square leg – and he should have been run out.

Malik, though, oozed class all through. Neil Foster and Gladstone Small were both below par, and Phillip DeFreitas (first five overs for 11) was understandably not the same bowler after he had gone off with a sudden bout of Delhi belly. Malik and Raja put on 167 in 29 overs before both were out shortly before the end.

From about 20 overs out, the crowd represented a more serious threat to Pakistan winning than England. There was one mini-riot, which held up play for about 10 minutes, and led to Gatting handing the umpire a chunk of rock that was not the kind with "Karachi" written right through it. After that, however, the only missiles came off the middle of the bat – and defeat had been inevitable long before it arrived with an over to spare.

Imran Khan bemoans his luck.

KARACHI SCOREBOARD

ENGLAND		PAKISTAN	
G A Gooch c Akram b Imran	16	Ramiz Raja c Gooch b DeFreitas	113
R T Robinson b Qadir	16	Mansoor Akhtar run out	29
C W J Athey b Tauseef	86	Salim Malik c Athey b Emburey	88
*M W Gatting c Yousuf b Qadir	60	Javed Miandad not out	6
A j Lamb b Imran	9	Ejaz Ahmed not out	4
J E Emburey lbw b Qadir	3	Extras (lb 6, w 1)	7
#P R Downton c Yousuf b Imran	6	Total (for 3, 49 overs)	247
N A Foster not out	20		
G C Small run out	0		
E E Hemmings not out	4		
Extras (lb 7, w 4)	11		
Total (9 wkts, 50 overs)	244		

Fall of wickets: 1-26, 2-52, 3-187, 4-187, 5-192, 6-203, 7-206. 8-230, 9-230.

Bowling: Imran 9-0-37-4, Akram 8-0-44-0, Tauseef 10-0-46-1, Qadir 10-0-31-3, Jaffer 8-0-44-0, Malik 5-0-35-0.

Fall of wickets: 1-61, 2-228, 3-243.

Did not bat: *Imran Khan, #Salim Yousuf Wasim Akram, Abdul Qadir, Tauseef Ahmed, Saleem Jaffer.

Bowling: DeFreitas 8-2-41-1, Foster 10-0-51-0, Hemmimgs 10-1-40-0, Emburey 10-0-34-1, Small 9-0-63-0, Gooch 2-0-12-0.

PAKISTAN WON BY 7 WICKETS

DATELINE, 22/10/87, MARTIN JOHNSON REPORTS . . .

SRI LANKA v WEST INDIES

England banking on a case of collapso

There was a time yesterday when it looked as though England might move a step nearer to qualification for the World Cup semi-finals without bowling a ball, but with the West Indies eventually withstanding a brave challenge from Sri Lanka in Kanpur, the battle to join Pakistan from Group B is now guaranteed to go right down to the wire.

However, nothing that England witnessed on their television sets in Karachi yesterday will have decreased their confidence for next Monday's showdown in Jaipur. At the moment, the Windies – mentally at any rate – look more like the kings of callapso than calypso.

Against the weakest attack in the tournament, they scored only 236 for 8 and the nerve-ends were visibly fraying during a Sri Lankan run-chase that ultimately failed only because of some amateur cricket in the final few overs.

Also, the West Indies' batting appears to be dangerously over-dependent on Viv Richards and Desmond Haynes, both of whom missed out yesterday, and they would have been in a fearful mess without an innings of 89 off 122 balls from the Trinidadian newcomer Phil Simmons.

They are also a long way short of the bowling side they were in each of the previous three World Cups, and their most experienced bowler out here, Courtney Walsh, has twice gone in the brain in crucial matches. He must be the only bowler to receive a special award (a Pakistan carpet) for effectively losing a match, and yesterday not even the fact that Sri Lanka required 28 runs could persuade Richards to entrust him with the final over again.

Walsh came in for more rough treatment in Kanpur, this time at the hands of the experienced left-hander, Arjuna Ranatunga, who made an unbeaten 87 off 92 balls and smashed Walsh for two sixes during the latter stages of Sri Lanka's run chase.

That helped bring a target of 87 from the final 10 overs with six wickets in hand down to an attainable 37 off 24 balls, but it was then that Ranatunga inherited a succession of dim-witted partners, who took it in turns to deprive him of the strike before then getting out.

Pakistan, meantime, cannot stop the money rolling in. The victory over England on Tuesday that guaranteed their semi-final place brought about the immediate bestowal (as it has after each of their victories) of what are described locally as "felicitations" from everyone from General Zia down to the local mayor.

England, who awarded themselves yesterday and today off, are now level on points with the West Indies, are not very far behind them on run rate, and even if they should lose in Jaipur, will retain an outside chance of qualififcation.

The West Indies would then have to lose their final match to Pakistan in Karachi on 30 October and England beat Sri Lanka – with a handsome total – in Pune on the same day.

If they beat the West Indies, on the other hand, a straightforward win over Sri Lanka – or even a two-points-apiece washout – would render the Karachi match irrelevant.

KANPUR SCOREBOARD

WEST INDIES

D Haynes b Anurasiri	24
P Simmons c Madugalle b J R Ratnayake	89
R Richardson c Mahanama b Jeganathan	4
*I V A Richards c R J Ratnayake b De Silva	14
G Logie not out	65
C Hooper st Kuruppu b De Silva	6
#J Dujon c Kuruppu b J R Ratnayake	6
R Harper b J R Ratnayake	3
W Benjamin b R J Ratnayake	0
C Walsh not out	9
Extras (b 2, lb 7, w 7)	16
Total (for 8, 50 overs)	236

Fall of wickets: 1-62, 2-80, 3-115, 4-155, 5-168, 6-199, 7-213, 8-214.
Did not bat: P Patterson.
Bowling: J R Ratnayake 10-1-41-3; John 5-1-25-0-; R J Ratnayake 5-0-39-1; Jeganathan 10-1-33-1; Anurasiri 10-1-46-1; De Silva 10-0-43-2.

SRI LANKA

R Mahanama b Patterson	0
#B Kuruppu c and b Hooper	33
J R Ratnayake lbw b Benjamin	15
R Madugalle c Haynes b Harper	18
A Ranatunga not out	86
*D Mendis b Walsh	19
A De Silva b Patterson	8
R J Ratnayake c Walsh b Patterson	5
S Jeganathan run out	3
V John not out	1
Extras (b 2, lb 11, nb 10)	23
Total (for 8, 50 overs)	211

Fall of wickets: 1-2, 2-28, 3-66, 4-86. 5-156, 6-184, 7-200, 8-209.
Did not bat: D Anurasiri
Bowling: Patterson 10-0-31-3; Walsh 9-2-43-1; Benjamin 10-0-43-1; Harper 10-1-29-1; Hooper 8-0-35-1; Richards 3-0-17-0.

WEST INDIES WON BY 25 RUNS

INDIA v AUSTRALIA

Maninder spins out Australia

It was spin bowling, traditionally India's most effective form of attack, which enabled them to beat Australia most convincingly, by 56 runs, in their return match in the World Cup qualifying round yesterday. India, who were put in, made 289 for 6 and Australia were then bowled out for 233 in the 49th over.

Australia and India are now level at the top of Group A with 12 points each and they are both fighting desperately to make sure they finish on top. The winners are assured of a semi-final in Bombay while the runners-up must travel to Lahore, which is an altogether less attractive option.

The pitch at the Kotla Stadium was flat and full of runs and the danger of putting the other side in was that they would score enough runs to shut their opponents out, which was exactly what India did, with four of their main batsmen scoring delightful half-centuries.

Australia began their innings at a tremendous rate, David Boon and Geoff Marsh putting on 89 in 18 overs. By then, Maninder Singh, at the

Navjot Sidhu waits the fall of the first wicket.

moment the best slow left-arm spinner in the world, had come on to bowl, and in his first eight overs he changed the course of the match.

He has matured and developed enormously in the last year or two and has become a most worthy successor to Bishen Bedi, a fellow Sikh.

Maninder has developed a lovely loop in his flight which was illustrated perfectly when he lured Marsh down the pitch and had him stumped by Kiran More with one which turned. Later in the innings both Allan Border, who was caught at long-on and Dean Jones, held at cover, also misjudged his flight.

He has become a real spinner of the ball, bowling across his braced front shoulder, and he drifted the ball cleverly into the right-hander. At present, he bowls everything from very wide of the crease. He needs to learn to vary his angle of delivery by using the width of the crease, for this will give him another important weapon.

Maninder came on to bowl the 16th over, when Boon and Marsh had been doing as they pleased with seam bowlers. The score was already 76, but in his second over Maninder disposed of Marsh and, bowling in tandem with his fellow left-arm spinner, Ravi Shastri, halted the flow of runs; suddenly, the Indians were in front.

The second Australian wicket fell to Shastri when Boon made room to cut and was caught behind. Boon, who never seems to think he is out, took an interminable time to leave the field and was loudly booed. As he came off, he made an unpleasant, bad-tempered gesture to the crowd and then had words with a group of spectators.

Border was third out at 135 and Maninder had taken 2 for 30 in eight overs. Kapil Dev now rested him for two overs and when he returned he at once got rid of Jones and Australia were 164 for four in the 36th over with the game lost.

The Kotla Stadium is much the smallest of the Indian Test grounds, being about the same size as Trent Bridge. With the short boundaries, the Australians decided not to risk either of their off-spinners on such a good pitch and their attack consisted of six seam bowlers. Neither of the Australians, Peter Tayor and Tim May, are in the same class as spin bowlers as Maninder but, even so, one at least would have lent a welcome variety to the attack. There was a boring sameness about the bowling and, after making such a defensive decision, maybe Australia deserved to lose.

Sunil Gavaskar and Kris Srikkanth gave India their usual *blitzkreig* stuff. Wonderful strokes came from both ends, and Srikkanth's square-drive off Bruce Reid was the pick of the bunch. Srikkanth then followed Craig McDermott's second ball and was caught behind.

Gavaskar and Navjot Sidhu continued the good work from India's point of view, although at a slightly less hectic rate. They both passed 50, and

Maninder Singh celebrates the stumping of Geoff Marsh.

when Gavaskar was bowled trying to run a ball to third man he left the Kotla Staium for the last time to suitably appreciative applause.

The innings faltered slightly in the middle when Sidhu and Kapil Dev threw their wickets away and Andrew Zesers bowled seven steady overs. But then Dilip Vengsarkar and Mohammad Azharuddin got going and it was then a question of whether or not India would reach 300. Azharuddin's strokes at the end were better than anyone's all day.

Sunil Gavaskar is bowled by O'Donnell.

NEW DELHI SCOREBOARD

INDIA	
K Srikkanth c Dyer b McDermott	26
Sunil Gavaskar b O'Donnell	61
Navjot Sidhu c Moody b McDermott	51
Dilip Vengsarkar c O'Donnell b Reid	63
*Kapil Dev c Dyer b McDermott	3
Mohammed Azharuddin not out	54
Ravi Shastri c and b Waugh	8
#Kiran More not out	5
Extras (1 b, 6 lb, 11 w)	18
Total (for 6, 50 overs)	**289**

Fall of wickets: 1-50, 2-125, 3-167, 4-178, 5-243, 6-271.

Did not bat: Prabhakar, Sharma, Maninder Singh.

Bowling: O'Donnell 9-1-45-1; Reid 10-0-65-1; Waugh 10-0-59-1; McDermott 10-0-61-3; Zesers 9-1-37-0; Moody 2-0-15-0.

INDIA WON BY 56 RUNS

AUSTRALIA	
G R Marsh st More b Maninder	33
D C Boon c More b Shastri	62
D M Jones c Dev b Maninder Singh	36
*A R Border c Prabhakar b Maninder Singh	12
S R Waugh c Sidhu b Kapil Dev	42
T W Moody run out	2
S P O'Donnell b Azharuddin	5
#G C Dyer c Dev b Prabhakar	15
C J McDermott c and b Azharuddin	4
A Zesers not out	2
B A Reid c Sidhu b Azharuddin	1
Extras (11 lb, 8 nb)	19
Total (49 overs)	**233**

Fall of wickets: 1-88, 2-104, 3-135, 4-164, 5-167, 6-182, 7-214, 8-227, 9-231.

Bowling: Kapil Dev 8-0-41-1; Prabhakar 10-0-56-1; Sharma 7.1-0-37-0; Maninder Singh 10-0-34-3; Shastri 10-0-35-1; Azharuddin 3.5-0-19-3.

NEW ZEALAND v ZIMBABWE

Crowes rescue the Kiwis

Although New Zealand beat Zimbabwe by four wickets at Eden Gardens, they could easily have lost. The Zimbabwe batsmen put up a much more convincing performance than of late, to reach 227 for 5, while the Kiwis needed the Crowe brothers to restore order after losing three quick wickets.

Zimbabwe's inspiration came from Kevin Arnott, the son of their manager, in only his second one-day international. After the opener Grant Paterson had been run out, Arnott and Ali Shah gave the innings a solid base and Arnott began to drive through the off-side and play off his legs in fine style as he found a stroke for almost every ball. He had just reached 51 when the bogged-down Ali Shah called him for a quick single then changed his mind and left his partner stranded.

New Zealand soon lost John Wright, Ken Rutherford and Dipak Patel, whose batting is becoming a big disappointment, but Martin Crowe reached 58 with an impressive array of strokes. After reaching 50, he swept Shah deep to square-leg, but in spite of losing Andrew Jones and Martin Snedden, Jeff Crowe then punished some wayward seam bowling in the closing overs and in the end New Zealand won without too much panic.

CALCUTTA SCOREBOARD

ZIMBABWE		NEW ZEALAND	
G A Paterson run out	0	K Rutherford b Brandes	22
Ali Shah c M Crowe b Watson	41	J Wright b Ali Shah	12
K J Arnott run out	51	M Crowe c Butchart b Ali Shah	58
#D L Houghton c M Crowe b Boock	50	Dipak Patel c Arnott b Butchart	1
A J Pycroft not out	52	*J Crowe not out	88
K M Curran b Boock	12	A Jones c Jarvis b Traicos	15
A C Waller not out	8	M Snedden b Jarvis	4
Extras (lb 7, w 6)	13	#I Smith not out	17
Total (for 5, 50 overs)	**227**	**Extras** (lb, 5 lb, 4 w, 1 nb)	11
		Total (for 6, 47.4 overs)	**228**

Fall of wickets: 1-1, 2-82, 3-121, 4-180, 5-216.

Did not Bat: Butchart, *Traicos, Brandes, Jarvis.

Bowling: Snedden 10-2-32-0; Chatfield 10-2-47-0; Patel 10-1-52-0; Boock 10-1-44-2; Watson 10-1-45-1.

Fall of wickets: 1-37, 2-53, 3-56, 4-125, 5-158, 6-182.

Did not bat: Watson, Boock, Chatfield.

Bowling: Curran 2-0-12-0; Jarvis 7.4-0-39-1; Brandes 10-1-44-2; Ali Shah 10-0-34-2; Traicos 10-0-43-1; Butchart 8-0-50-0.

NEW ZEALAND WON BY 4 WICKETS

DATELINE JAIPUR, 24/10/87, MARTIN JOHNSON REPORTS...

England ready to save their bacon

Five victories in six one-day internationals against the West Indies in less than a year is an impressive record by any standards, but unless England can make it six out of seven in Jaipur on Monday, their prospects of advancing to the knockout stages in this World Cup will be hovering somewhere between slim and none.

For what it's worth, England will have a good luck message from Pakistan in their corner for this one – albeit only because Imran wants the West Indies out of the way, for an hour of Viv Richards can win any match. However, England's more solid all-round strength should still make them marginal favourites in Jaipur.

The West Indies may also be just a little suspect in terms of morale. The sub-continent is a fascinating place, but it's not exactly fun, fun, fun all the way when the sun goes down. It's the same for both sides, of course, but it's amazing how an English man's flagging spirit can be revived by simple things, such as arriving in India from Pakistan and being able to get a bacon sandwich for breakfast, or, in the captain's case, someone flying out with a fresh jar of Branston.

Mike Gatting has also been perked up by the recent discovery of a pair of missing boots. They turned up inside one of the team's tuck boxes, so it was either a packing error, or else commendable foresight from someone who knew it was the one place the skipper was sure to look.

There is also a marked difference in appraisal between the respective camps as to how they've lost both their group matches to date. The West

Indies captain has marked it down more to bad luck than bad cricket – there were so many "ifs" flying around yesterday no-one was quite sure whether the quotes had come from Viv Richards or Rudyard Kipling – but England have at least pleaded guilty in one or two areas, and set about working on them.

Micky Stewart described fielding in the latter stages of the second Pakistan game as "the worst under pressure I can remember in the past 12 months", and there was a heavy accent on fielding during yesterday's practise. Stewart has also spoken to Bill Athey about the reverse sweep shot that precipitated the collapse at Karachi.

Both sides are likely to show a couple of changes from their Gujranwala meeting. For the West Indies, Phil Simmons has now established himself as a much brighter batting prospect than Carlisle Best and Tony Gray, who has yet to play in this competition – presumably because of the absence of bounce in the pitches – should come in this time. It may be at the expense of Courtney Walsh, as Richards is rather keen to see an absence of bounce from the third tier of the stand during the 50th over.

Pringle and Robinson, both of whom played in Gujranwala, look like being left out for Monday's return encounter. Pringle's bowling has been such that he can be considered only as a batsman, and his batting has been such that he can be considered only as a bowler. *Ergo*, carry on Eddie Hemmings, and with Athey having established himself in Karachi, it remains to be seen whether Broad will return at Robinson's expense.

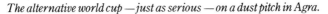

The alternative world cup — just as serious — on a dust pitch in Agra.

Pace still dominates in the West Indian attack, although in the absence of Marshall (with him here they'd now have four wins out of four) and Garner, things are certainly not what they used to be. Not one of the current crop of bowlers would make it into a World Cup Select XI, whereas at least three would have been automatic choices in each of the three previous competitions.

Imran, Akram and Qadir would walk in, which is why Pakistan have emerged as such strong favourites. Something else about them emerged yesterday which, on reflection, means we might have been a little harsh on Javed Miandad for his petulant reaction on being given out lbw in the first England game in Rawalpindi. The Australian umpire Tony Crafter, whose decision sparked it all off, later discovered that it was the first time Javed had been given out leg before in international cricket in his own country.

So now we know why the poor lad was so upset. It wasn't because he thought there had been a poor interpretation of law 36 but simply because he was unaware of its existence.

DATELINE JAIPUR, 26/10/87, MARTIN JOHNSON REPORTS . . .

England cast into the cold

Such has been the success of the sub-continent's first World Cup that England, who staged the first three tournaments, might find themselves frozen out as hosts until the turn of the century.

India and Pakistan estimate that, quite apart from having developed at least half a dozen new venues capable of staging international cricket, they'll make so many rupees from this year's event that they want it back again in 1991 and 1995.

Pakistan have already unearthed a sponsor for the next one and lodged a concrete bid with the ICC. And yesterday they announced that whatever the offer from any other country, they would top it by 25 per cent.

At the moment, there is a chance of one of the next two tournaments becoming something like the Fosters or XXXX World Cup. The Australian board are conducting a feasibility study (ie, is there anybody with a bottomless bucket of dollars in exchange for a plug?), but one thing is certain, Pakistan and India will not be too heartbroken to lose out to Australia, but anything is better than England getting their hands on it again.

They still imagine that our game is run by the MCC, and (more perceptively this time) that the MCC is made up of megalomaniacs wearing egg and bacon ties who possess Doctor Strangelove ideas of world domination.

England received some idea of how meticulously the host nations have prepared for their big moment when they arrive in Jaipur for today's match against the West Indies. This historic town hasn't had a monsoon in five years, yet they've spent a fortune on making sure that the cricket ground has enough water on tap to be able to stage a regatta at the flick of a switch.

In Rawalpindi, houses were demolished to increase spectator capacity, and in Jaipur, the stadium has been given an extensive facelift since England were last here in 1984-85. Facilities at the grounds are generally first-class, but if there is an area in which they've been caught just a touch unawares, it's in communications. British Telecom might drive you mad, but a box of homing pigeons is an essential accessory in Peshawar, and one harrassed correspondent has been phoning his copy from Jaipur to a housewife in Surrey.

However, things eventually do get done, always with a smile, and always at their own pace. No one swears or shakes a fist, content in the knowledge that sooner or later (almost always later) they'll get there.

So they did at the ground yesterday. In mid-morning the boundary markings were 60 yards away instead of the mandatory 75, and there was constant threat of treading in freshly-mixed cement or a pot of gloss paint. It was as if they'd only been informed about the World Cup over breakfast, but by the end of the day, it looked as though it had been ready since the days of top hats and curved bats.

Tony Gray, the West Indian fast bowler. Gray was forced to miss today's match against England after breaking his arm during practise. Gray was struck just above the left wrist while batting in the nets against medium-pace bowler Carl Hooper.

DATELINE 26/10/87, FROM OUR CORRESPONDENT...

PAKISTAN v SRI LANKA

Pakistan led by art of Malik

Pakistan completed the formality of winning their World Cup group by sweeping aside Sri Lanka in Faisalabad yesterday. Led by a maiden one-day international century by Salim Malik, Pakistan made 297 for 7 and restricted Sri Lanka to 184 for 8 in their 50 overs, to win by 113 runs. The victory ensures that Pakistan's semi-final will be played in Lahore.

FAISALABAD SCOREBOARD

PAKISTAN		SRI LANKA	
Rameez Raja c and b Anurasiri	32	R Mahanama run out	8
Mansoor Akhtar b Jeganathan	33	#B Kuruppu c Yousuf b Imran	0
Salim Malik b Ratnayake	100	J R Ratnayake run out	22
Javed Miandad run out	1	R Madugalle c Yousuf b Manzoor Elahi	15
Wasim Akram c Ranatunga b De Silva	39	A Ranatunga c and b Qadir	50
Ijaz Ahmed c and b John	30	*D Mendis b Qadir	58
*Imran Khan run out	39	A De Silva not out	13
Manzoor Elahi not out	4	A De Mel b Qadir	0
#Salim Yousuf not out	11	S Jeganathan c Yousuf b Miandad	1
Extras (b 6, w 2)	8	V John not out	1
Total (for 7, 50 overs)	297	Extras (b 4, lb 4, nb 2, w 6)	16
		Total (for 8, 50 overs)	184

Fall of wickets: 1-64, 2-72, 3-77, 4-137, 5-197, 6-264, 7-285.
Did not bat: Tauseef, Qadir.
Bowling: Ratnayake 10-0-58-1; John 8-1-53-1; De Mel 10-0-53-0; Jeganathan 9-1-45-1; Anurasiri 7-0-45-1; De Silva 6-0-37-1.

Fall of wickets: 1-4, 2-11, 3-41, 4-70, 5-150, 6-173, 7-173, 8-179.
Did not bat: Anurasiri
Bowling: Imran 3.2-1-13-1; Akram 7-0-34-0; Elahi 9.4-0-32-1; Tauseef 10-1-23-0; Qadir 10-0-40-3; Malik 7-1-29-0; Miandad 3-0-5-1.

PAKISTAN WON BY 113 RUNS

DATELINE JAIPUR, 27/10/87, MARTIN JOHNSON REPORTS . . .

ENGLAND v WEST INDIES

Hemmings sets up a fireworks party

Unless England lose to Sri Lanka in Pune on Friday (improbable) and the West Indies beat Pakistan in Karachi (on current form, unlikely), yesterday's 34-run victory at Jaipur will confirm England as runners-up in by far the tougher of the two groups and book them a place in the Bombay semifinal on Guy Fawkes Day. Fireworks guaranteed – and if it's against India, literally.

This was the 29th meeting between England and the West Indies in one-day internationals, and on no previous occasion had England scored more than 252. Yesterday they topped that by 17 runs – thanks in no small measure to the opposition donating so many extra deliveries that the England innings came close to being played under Benson and Hedges rules – and yet the game appeared to be slipping irretrievably away until one of sport's unlikelier took a hand.

With Viv Richards having just engaged full throttle, he stepped back to cut a delivery from Eddie Hemmings, the rotund Nottinghamshire off-spinner, that was heading for his stumps, and English joy was unconfined when the great man missed it.

The match turned sharply (even if the ball did not) there and then, and everything that occurred thereafter confirmed how overdependent the West Indies are on Richards, and how suspect their temperaments can be if he gets out. A target of 65 from the final 10 overs, with only four men out, and Richards there to oversee things, would have been almost routine. However, while Viv was back in the shower, England cleaned up the last six wickets for only 30, and Hemmings played another decisive part when his direct hit from 30 yards ran out Roger Harper. Harper running out Hemmings would scarcely have been news, but this really was man bites dog.

Looking at it more broadly, the West Indies were undone by squandering the first toss of real importance we had seen in the competition. The pitch was unusually well grassed, and shortly before the 9am start there was still so much dew on the outfield ("lapping over my wellies", was one reporter's verdict) that there was clearly some moisture in the pitch too. There was also bounce, and had it been a Test match with Marshall and Garner around, you would not have backed England to survive until tea.

The West Indies, however, clearly cannot come to terms with the shoulder-high bouncer-rule refinement, and Patrick Patterson – probably

Viv Richards takes a drink.

on automatic pilot – promptly gave away two wides with bouncers. If horizontal inaccuracy was understandable, the lateral variety was not.

Eventually, West Indies conceded the alarming total of 22 wides, which would have been a hapless performance even for the Sri Lanka attack, and heaven knows how many dodgy ones the umpires half-twitched at before deciding to give the benefit of the doubt to the bowler. England's eventual extras' total of 38 was even better than their winning margin.

Some of the fielding wasn't much better, and both Tim Robinson (retained only marginally, one imagines, ahead of Chris Broad) and Bill Athey survived early chances to Phillip Dujon behind the stumps. Robinson finally had his off stump snapped in half after 36 minutes, but each minute he lasted while the West Indies (Courtney Walsh excepted) were misusing steadily-improving conditions was precious.

Carl Hooper, who took three high-ranking England wickets in Gujranwala – Gatting, Gooch and Pringle (OK, make that two-and-a-half), wasn't so much inaccurate as unable to identify the pitch – and after three abysmal overs, Richards had to make an unrehearsed appearance with his flat off-spin. He did an excellent job too, because Graham Gooch, who was in lovely touch, and Mike Gatting were beginning to capitalise handsomely on a fast start when Richards pulled them up sharply.

England were 150 for 2 at 30 overs, having added 71 in the previous 10, when Richards had Gatting leg-before sweeping in the 31st. The effect was such that only 35 runs came between the 30th and 40th overs, with Lamb giving a fair old demonstration of why he is flying home after the first leg of the winter treble. He was barely able to get Richards off the square, which suggests that he has trouble not only with spinners, but also with slow bowlers who don't spin it.

Lamb did more damage against the quicks, and England recovered with 83 off the final overs. John Emburey was in the thick of it as usual, practising orthodox strokes at the non-striker's end and playing bizarre ones at the business end. Gooch just missed a well-deserved century (135 balls, seven fours), and DeFreitas also clubbed away to good effect.

Despite what has happened to Walsh in previous games, quite why Richards should instead have employed Benjamin – who ended the summer in Leicestershire's second XI – to bowl at the death, is not easily explained.

Richard, though, might have clawed it all back after a bizarre start to the West Indian innings, when they appeared to be trying to get the runs in about 15 overs. This may not have been unconnected with Neil Foster's opening spell, in which he was unable to bowl anything other than the unplayable delivery and the unspeakable delivery.

At halfway, the West Indies were almost on par with England's impressive rate of progress, with Richie Richardson having finally come through

Graham Gooch — man of the match.

one of the worst half-centuries he will ever make and Richards having just embarked on what threatened to be a ritual execution of both spinners. Emburey had gone for one massive six, and Hemmings two more in consecutive deliveries. But once the general had departed, a long procession of privates shot themselves one by one in the foot.

At the awards ceremony (at which Gooch took the medal which probably belonged to Hemmings) was the newly-arrived England chairman Peter May. It's a moot point as to whether England were inspired because of him, or in spite of him, but either way it represented their most important victory for quite a time.

JAIPUR SCOREBOARD

ENGLAND

G A Gooch c Harper b Patterson 92
R T Robinson b Patterson 13
C W J Athey c Patterson b Harper 21
*M W Gatting lbw b Richards 25
A J Lamb c Richardson b Patterson 40
J E Emburey not out 24
P A J DeFreitas not out 16
Extras (b 5, lb 10, w 22, nb 1) 38
Total (for 5, 50 overs) 269

Fall of wickets: 1 .35. 2-90, 3-154, 4-209, 5-250.
Did not bat: #P R Downton, N A Foster, E E Hemmings, G C Small.
Bowling: Patterson 9-0-56-3; Walsh 10-0-24-0; Benjamin 10-0-63-0; Harper 10-1-52-1; Hooper 3-0-27-0; Richards 8-0-32-1.

ENGLAND WON BY 34 RUNS.

WEST INDIES

D L Haynes c Athey b DeFreitas 9
P V Simmons b Emburey 25
R B Richardson c Downton b Small 93
*I V A Richards b Hemmings 51
A L Logie c Hemmings b Emburey 22
C L Hooper c Downton b DeFreitas 8
#P J Dujon c Downton b Foster 1
R A Harper run out 3
W K M Benjamin c Foster b DeFreitas 8
C A Walsh b Hemmings 2
B P Patterson not out 4
Extras (lb 7, w 1, nb 1) 9
Total (48.1 overs) 235

Fall of wickets: 1-18, 2-65, 3-147, 4-182, 5-208, 6-211, 7-219, 8-221, 9-224.
Bowling: DeFreitas 9.1-2-28-3; Foster 10-0-52-1; Emburey 9-0-41-2; Small 10-0-61-1; Hemmings 10-0-46-2.

INDIA v ZIMBABWE
Indians ignore captain's orders

India beat Zimbabwe without any apparent difficulty by seven wickets with eight overs to spare, but inexplicably they made no obvious attempt to score their runs fast enough to boost their run-rate so that they finish ahead of Australia in Group A.

As it is, Australia, who have won three games with two to play, against New Zealand and Sri Lanka, are still fractionally ahead of India, who have only New Zealand to play.

Unless New Zealand beat Australia, it looks as if Australia will end up as the winners of Group A in which case they will play England in the semifinal in Bombay. If India finish second, as now seems probable, they will have the unenviable task of taking on Pakistan in Lahore.

The Indian batsmen failed to respond to Kapil Dev's urging that they score the runs required to beat Zimbabwe in 38 overs or less. Sunil Gavaskar took 35 overs over his 50. "Twice I sent messages to step up the scoring rate, but he did not," said Kapil. "I am disappointed with Gavaskar."

After being put in to bat, Zimbabwe reached 191 for 7, which was never likely to be enough, although Kevin Arnott made a well-ordered 60. Both Navjot Sidhu and Gavaskar reached 50 for India before Kapil and Dilip Vengsarkar finished the job, taking India to 194 for 8 in 42 overs.

Zimbabwe's innings had begun with the obligatory run-out before they had reached double figures and then Arnott, David Houghton and Andrew Waller batted well enough to suggest that if they had had more practice against top-class bowling, Zimbabwe might have come close to holding their own in this company.

For once, India were given a less-than-hectic start by Gavaskar and Kris Srikkanth. For a while Sidhu increased the pace, but in the circumstances there was an extraordinary lack of urgency about India's batting.

AHMEDABAD SCOREBOARD

ZIMBABWE

R D Brown c More b Sharma	13
Ali Shah run out	0
K Arnott b Kapil Dev	60
A J Pycroft c More b Sharma	2
#D L Houghton c Kapil Dev b Shastri	22
A C Waller c Shastri b Maninder	39
I P Butchart b Kapil Dev	13
P W E Rawson not out	16
E Brandes not out	3
Extras (b 1, lb 12, w 9, nb 1)	23
Total (for 7, 50 overs)	191

Fall of wickets: 1-4, 2-36, 3-40, 4-83, 5-150, 6-155, 7-184.

Did not bat: M P Jarvis, *A J Traicos.

Bowling: Kapil Dev 10-2-44-2; Prabhakar 7-2-12-0; Sharma 10-0-41-2; Maninder 10-1-32-1; Shastri 10-0-35-1; Azharuddin 3-0-14-0.

INDIA

K Srikkanth lbw b Jarvis	6
S M Gavaskar c Butchart b Rawson	50
N S Sidhu c Brandes b Rawson	55
D B Vengsarkar not out	33
*Kapil Dev not out	9
Extras (lbw 6, w 3)	9
Total (for 3, 42 overs)	194

Fall of wickets: 1-11, 2-105, 3-132.

Did not bat: M Azharuddin, R J Shastri, #K S More, M Prabhakar, Chetan Sharma, Maninder Singh.

Bowling: Jarvis 8-1-21-1; Rawson 8-0-46-2; Brandes 6-0-28-0; Traicos 10-0-39-0; Shah 8-0-40-0; Butchart 2-0-14-0.

INDIA WON BY 7 WICKETS

DATELINE, 28/10/87, MARTIN JOHNSON REPORTS...

Belated logic puts heart into England

So far in this World Cup England have not lost to anybody other then themselves, and as long as they remember to take a syringe-full of over-confidence vaccine along with all their other pills and potions, their provisional booking for the Bombay semi-final will not be threatened by Sri Lanka in their final Group B match at Pune on Friday.

Ever since the World Cup draw was made it has been difficult to shake off the sneaking suspicion that the Sri Lankans might just cause one upset before flying home, but such was England's efficiency against the West Indies in Jaipur that an 11th-hour upset is unthinkable.

Even then it would require a substantial West Indian victory over Pakistan in Karachi to deprive them on run-rate, and Monday's events in Jaipur would suggest that the West Indies are too far "gone" at all levels, including that part of the body in which 90 per cent of this game is played – the head – to cheat the hangman now.

The England management are sensibly not taking the Sri Lankans for granted, and there is a slightly worrying variety of aches, pain and strains in the camp, most notably affecting Gooch, Small and Emburey. However, leaving aside the constant worry about illness, everyone is expected to be fit for Pune, and the England manager Micky Stewart says he wants "the strongest available side for a vital match".

This would seem a pointer against giving Paul Jarvis his first match, although as Stewart's pre-Jaipur comments erroneously led us to suspect Broad's return for Robinson, Jarvis may not be entirely out of the running.

Perhaps the most pleasing aspect of Monday's win was the confirmation that the tour selectors are beginning to apply a spot of belated logic to the situation. Early on, there is no way that Eddie Hemmings would have been selected ahead of Derek Pringle on a pitch with both grass and bounce, but Hemming's performance was a mini-triumph for the old adage that you pick your best bowlers regardless of conditions.

England are still not an outstanding side – the absence of Botham and Gower combined with an absence of common sense from the original selection panel saw to that – but they are solidly professional to a man, and Stewart and Mike Gatting have repeated last winter's achievement over morale.

Fielding that had previously fluctuated between the barely acceptable and the geriatric, was significantly better in Jaipur, and it has also become even clearer that Leicestershire will have to conduct a serious inquest into why Phillip DeFreitas's heart pumps twice as fiercely when he exchanges the running fox for the three lions.

Graham Gooch, unhappy with last season's form for Essex, is nonetheless in splendid form here, Bill Athey has (for the moment anyway) obviated the need for Gatting to move up to No. 3, and Paul Downton has been particularly sharp behind the stumps.

The long-range forecast for England is, however, not good – if the astrologer commissioned by one local newspaper a week or so ago has got it right. Not surprisingly, the stars have a patriotic look, but his semi-final predictions may well work out: England v India in Bombay and

Paul Downton rises to the occasion.

Pakistan v Australia in Lahore. From then on it's bad news. India to beat Pakistan in the final.

If he's right, the boys from the Met office might do well to give him a ring the next time they're considering issuing a "may be a touch on the windy side this evening" type of forecast. Our man in Delhi, spot on with his "no monsoon this year" prediction, also advertises himself as a hurricane specialist.

DATELINE CHANDIGARH, 28/10/87, HENRY BLOFELD REPORTS...

AUSTRALIA v NEW ZEALAND
Marsh kills off the Kiwis

New Zealand are out of the World Cup and at the last they had only themselves to blame for some unprofessional cricket. Australia, who won the toss, reached 251 for 8 having looked for 40 overs like having to settle for significantly less.

But Geoff Marsh battled brilliantly for his century, showing great stamina in high heat and humidity. He took a severe toll of Ewen Chatfield, who inexplicably bowled the last over at Marsh's legs. It cost New Zealand 19 runs, and in the end Australia won by 17 runs.

In the first part of the day Australia did not score fast enough to keep their run-rate ahead of India, who lead the group. The final two games will decide who finish top and play their semi-final in Bombay, and who will have to travel to Lahore. Australia face Zimbabwe while India take on New Zealand, which ought to give Australia the advantage.

It was a good, if slow pitch, and David Boon and Marsh seemed about to give Australia their usual excellent start when Marsh pushed Chatfield into the covers. Boon set off and was stranded when sent back. This brought in Dean Jones and he and Marsh now put on 126 in 26 overs.

It was a good stand, even if it never really got on top of the bowling, and it was broken in the 36th over when, after picking up Willie Watson off his legs for six, Jones drove at the next ball without much footwork and was caught behind.

The middle order now collapsed. Allan Border drove Martin Snedden into his stumps, Mike Veletta ran himself out first ball, Waugh drove all round Chatfield and Australia were struggling. It was left to Marsh – who had reached his fourth one-day international hundred – to take advantage of Chatfield in his inexplicable closing overs.

The two left-handers, John Wright and Snedden, gave New Zealand a good start, scoring 72 in 17 overs, before Snedden was out, closely followed by Martin Crowe, who was unluckily dismissed when Wright drove

Steve Waugh powerfully back down the pitch and the bowler deflected it on to the stumps with Crowe out of his ground backing up.

Wright went on to reach 50 but resorted to desperate measures too soon and gave Zesers an easy return catch. Jeff Crowe's only idea seemed to be to make room and cut the off-spinners from in front of leg-stump. He had got most of his 27 runs this way before giving Border a simple return catch.

Ken Rutherford played some brave strokes before hooking to deep find-leg. New Zealand were then 179 for 5 in the 40th over and in spite of some hopeful hitting by the tailenders their chance had gone. Without Richard Hadlee they were always going to struggle in this competition, and so it has proved.

CHANDIGARH SCOREBOARD

AUSTRALIA

G R Marsh not out	126
D C Boon run out	14
D M Jones c Smith b Watson	56
*A R Border b Snedden	1
M R J Veletta run out	0
S R Waugh b Watson	1
#G C Dyer b Chatfield	8
C J McDermott lbw b Chatfield	5
T B A May run out	15
A K Zesers not out	8
Extras (lb 10, w 7)	17
Total (for 8, 50 overs)	251

Fall of wickets: 1-25, 2-151, 3-158, 4-158. 5-175, 6-193, 7-201, 8-228.
Did not bat: B A Reid.
Bowling: Snedden 10-0-48-1, Chatfield 10-2-52-2; Boock 10-1-45-0; Bracewell 4-0-24-0; Patel 8-0-26-0; Watson 8-0-46-2.

NEW ZEALAND

M C Snedden b Waugh	32
J G Wright c and b Zesers	61
M D Crowe run out	4
K R Rutherford c Jones b McDermott	44
*J J Crowe c and b Border	27
D N Patel st Dyer b Border	3
J G Bracewell run out	12
#I D S Smith c Boon b Waugh	12
S L Boock run out	12
W Watson run out	8
E J Chatfield not out	5
Extras (b 1, lb 7, w 4, nb 2)	14
Total (48. 4 overs)	234

Fall of wickets: 1-72, 2-82, 3-127, 4-173, 5-179, 6-186, 7-206, 8-208, 9-221.
Bowling: McDermott 10-1-43-1; Reid 6-0-30-0; Waugh 9.4-0-37-2; Zesers 67-0-37-1; May 10-0-52-0; Border 7-0-27-2.

AUSTRALIA WON BY 17 RUNS

Jarvis takes on the Lucan role

Every England tour seems to throw up its Lord Lucan, the two most recent being Les Taylor in the West Indies and Wilf Slack in Australia. Taylor even looked like him – or at least looked like what he used to look like.

At the moment, that dubious distinction belongs to the Yorkshire fast bowler Paul Jarvis, who is bearing up to anonymity with equanimity, fortified perhaps by the knowledge that his winter will have a good more meaning as soon as this World Cup is over.

Unless forced to do so by injuries or illness, England will not pick him for a single competitive game until they begin their three-Test tour of Pakistan – always assuming that Jarvis has not by then contracted a terminal case of agoraphobia and is unable to bowl anywhere other than inside a net.

As it happens, Jarvis virtually ruled himself out of contention for England's final World Cup group match against Sri Lanka in Pune tomorrow after bowling for only 15 minutes during yesterday's practice before having a cortisone injection in the shoulder that has been bothering him on and off since the start of the tour.

Had it not been for that, there would have been a strong case for his inclusion against the Sri Lankans, possibly at the expense of Gladstone Small, whose last 19 World Cup overs have cost him 124 runs, and who is struggling for full fitness himself. Small has been afflicted by mysterious shooting pains in his right forearm that occur occasionally during delivery, and more often when throwing.

England, though, as manager Micky Stewart more or less conceded a couple of times this week, would not have seriously included Jarvis in their World Cup strategy, fit or otherwise.

There are two reasons for this. Firstly, when it comes to team selection, England's traditional motto has always been to let boldness be someone else's friend; and secondly, their original selection for the World Cup was a triumph for muddled thinking.

Jarvis's inexperience at international level (none) always made it improbable that he would be blooded in anything other than a dead match before the Pakistan and New Zealand tours; Derek Pringle's problems have not exactly come as a surprise; and there was never going to be a situation in which Tim Robinson, Chris Broad and Bill Athey were all going to be chosen together in a 50-over contest. Ergo, England are now effectively selecting from 11.

Also, it required no great foresight to predict that 50-over matches – forced by the sudden loss of daylight at around 5 o'clock on the subcontinent – would be entirely different to those played over 60. So by leaving behind such players as Ashley Metcalfe, Neil Fairbrother, Wayne Larkins and Peter Willey, the onus of scoring runs at a brisk rate from the start has fallen on just three front-line batsmen – Graham Gooch, Mike Gatting and Allan Lamb.

Fortunately for England, all three have been in excellent form, which is why Lamb will probably play in Pune despite the fact that he has a similar shoulder injury to Jarvis. It may, however, mean that Lamb will not be able to field out in the deep, where no one other than Phillip DeFreitas can match him for his combination of throwing arm and mobility.

Lamb was unable to practice yesterday, and John Emburey, Eddie Hemmings, Athey and Gatting all took a precautionary day off, too, because of various slight niggles. It was, however, an impressive session in that (and one wonders why it has not happened before) it bore much more relation to match conditions than is normally the case.

The bowlers operated in pairs, six balls on, six balls off, which was also beneficial in enabling the batsmen to develop a more realistic rhythm. Usually they end up getting something like 20 deliveries a minute from all manner of bowlers, and, as amateur golfers will know, whacking away at a box off 100 balls down at the driving range becomes, after a time, a sure-fire recipe for perfecting the duff and the shank.

England should have only one real selection poser in Pune, whether to recall Broad in place of Robinson, who was dropped off nervous edges early on in both the previous two group matches. Broad's form in the nets has been patchy, to say the least, but he is so much sounder against real pace than Robinson that if England were not happy about recalling him for the West Indies, it is difficult to see how they can now make out a case for him in this one.

Assuming England win tomorrow – and Sri Lanka's English coach Don Smith is among those who will be staggered if they do not ("Our lads were shattered by England's sheer professionalism in the first group game") – nothing the West Indies do against Pakistan in Karachi can prevent their advancing into the semi-finals.

Then on Saturday England will doubtless be tuned in to the live television coverage from Nagpur of India, versus New Zealand, which will decide whether India or Australia meet them as winners of Group A. As this will be played in Bombay, one imagines England would much prefer Australia.

DATELINE PUNE, 30/10/87, MARTIN JOHNSON REPORTS . . .

England fly in for a net loss

If England's tour doctor prescribed a double dose of nerve tonic last night, it probably had more to do with the usual kamikaze aeroplane ride and Pune's coconut-shy net facilities than any attack of the jitters about today's final Group B match against Sri Lanka.

Air travel on the sub-continent is, as they say, something else. Last year a PIA trainee pilot failed to satisfy the examiner when he put his passengers down in Islamabad without engaging the landing gear. By comparison, England's short hop from Bombay to Pune wasn't in the same league – but after the customary three-hour delay for a 25-minute trip, the players didn't exactly need the pilot to overshoot the runway before getting it right the second time.

England then took one look at the nets in Pune's Gandhi Stadium and concluded the pilot and groundsman must be one and the same person. Mike Gatting's summing-up was along the lines of "death-trap" and he took the team to the nearby Poona (they retained the old spelling) Club.

Conditions there were not much better and England soon gave up after Bill Athey retired with a damaged thumb and Phillip DeFreitas was in a freak accident similar to the one that befell Paul Downton in Jaipur.

England's net sessions are invariably attended by an enthusiastic band of ball-fetchers and one high-velocity return from a young Indian volunteer struck DeFreitas on the shoulder just as he was about to bowl. He was more shocked than seriously hurt, although he trudged off to the pavilion muttering something about taking up a less dangerous sport.

DATELINE PUNE, 31/10/87, MARTIN JOHNSON REPORTS . . .

ENGLAND v SRI LANKA
Gooch takes lead in England routine

You could have cut the tension with, well, half a pound of lard actually. The gulf in class was yawning (as were we all by the end) and England eventually collected their 5 November semi-final place in Bombay with eight wickets and 52 balls to spare.

There was always the suspicion that Sri Lanka might have been capable of springing a surprise in Group B, but in the event they've performed more like plankton than minnows, and England's victory in Pune yesterday was every bit as routine as the one in Peshawar.

It wasn't much of a spectacle for the crowd – whose quest for entertainment at one point manifested itself in lobbing empty cans at Derek Pringle while he was on boundary patrol dispensing drinks to thirsty fielders – and England's one real danger was over-confidence.

They would have made it with even greater ease had they not helped inflate Sri Lanka's total with a series of fielding lapses. However, 218 was still hopelessly inadequate for a halfway decent attack to defend, never mind Sri Lanka's. The pitch offered nothing but very occasional slow turn, and while the outfield resembled a cabbage patch, it might well have been made of polished porcelain from the way the ball flew across it.

The possibility of England's getting mugged, as it were, a couple of yards from the bank, occurred just once, during the very first over. Phillip DeFreitas's opening delivery was a leg-stump half-volley that Mahanama put away for four, and his fifth resulted not only in the first of four dropped catches, but also in a dislocated finger for Graham Gooch. However, while Gooch was off the field for most of the innings, physiotherapist Laurie Brown not only got him fit to bat, but bat well enough to end up with the man of the match award.

Paul Jarvis (on at the time for Gooch) and Paul Downton (twice) also dropped catches, by far the most expensive being the first of Downton's, when Roy Dias had made only a single.

The 35-year-old Sri Lankan vice-captain, who had not played since being dropped after the opening group match, went on to make 80 off 117 balls, including six fours, and three of his team's five leg-side sixes.

England – and Foster in particular – gave Sri Lanka rather too much scope to play off their legs, the major beneficiaries, during a third-wicket partnership of 88 in 22 overs, being Dias and Gurusingha. The innings, though, stagnated again when they were involved in one of those comic mix-ups that ends up in someone (Gurusingha in this case) run out by yards going for the single when he might conceivable have run two.

A late flourish produced 74 from the final 10 overs, but any doubts about Gooch's finger were dispelled when the first ball of England's innings was shelled to the mid-off boundary, and while Robinson – again preferred to Broad – may have his problems against the quick, short stuff, he is a class performer against anything else.

As Sri Lanka's batsmen would score 300 every time against their own bowlers, all Gooch and Robinson had to overcome was the monotony of scoring easy runs. Even their regular mid-pitch conferences must have been born of habit rather than necessity, unless of course they were merely sorting out a game of golf for today's rest day.

In the end neither quite managed to concentrate hard enough to see it through by themselves. Robinson was bowled sweeping and Gooch, having earlier survived a difficult chance to mid-wicket, was quietly attempting to milk his umpteenth leg-side single when he got a leading edge back to the bowler.

Gooch's 60 from 79 balls (Robinson made 55 off 74) was none the less enough to win – in what must have been a photofinish from Dias – his second consecutive man of the match medal. Now England await either Australia or India in Bombay, and at this stage they'd justifiably fancy their chances against either.

PUNE SCOREBOARD

SRI LANKA

R Mahanama c Emburey b DeFreitas 14
J R Ratnayake lbw b Small 7
#A Gurusingha run out 34
R Dias st Downton b Hemmings 80
*D Mendis b DeFreitas 7
R Madugalle c sub b Hemmings 22
A de Silva not out 23
A de Mel c Lamb b Hemmings 0
S Jeganathan not out 20
Extras (lb 3, w 3, nb 5) 11
Total (for 7, 50 overs) **218**

Fall of wickets: 1-22, 2-25, 3-113, 4-125, 5-170,
6-171, 7-180.
Did not bat: V John, D Anurasiri.
Bowling: DeFreitas 10-2-46-2; Small
10-1-33-1; Foster 10-0-37-0; Emburey
10-1-42-0; Hemmings 10-1-57-3.

ENGLAND

G A Gooch c and b Jeganathan 61
R T Robinson b Jeganathan 55
C W J Athey not out 40
*M W Gatting not out 46
Extras (b 1, lb 13, w 3) 17
Total (for 2, 41.2 overs) **219**

Fall of wickets: 1-123, 2-132.
Did not bat: A J Lamb, J E Emburey, #P R
Downton, P A J DeFreitas, N A Foster, E E
Hemmings, G C Small.
Bowling: Ratnayake 8-1-7-0; John 6-2-19-0; De
Mel 4.2-0-34-0; Jeganathan 10-0-45-2;
Anurasiri 10-0-45-0; De Silva 3-0-25-0.

ENGLAND WON BY 8 WICKETS

DATELINE DELHI, 31 /10 /87, HENRY BLOFELD REPORTS . . .

AUSTRALIA v ZIMBABWE

Australia left in suspense

Australia were left with an anxious wait to find out which semi-final they
will be in, after only marginally improving their run-rate in a 70-run win
against Zimbabwe in New Delhi.

Their total of 266 for 5 edged their only slightly pst India, who play
New Zealand today. The winners of the group will play England in Bombay, with the losers facing Pakistan in Lahore.

David Boon and Dean Jones looked to have set up a big total, but tidy
bowling and superb fielding pegged them back.

NEW DELHI SCOREBOARD

AUSTRALIA

G R Marsh run out 37
D C Boon c Houghton b Butchart 93
D M Jones not out 58
C J McDermott c Rawson b Traicos 9
*A R Border st Houghton b Traicos 4
M R J Veletta run out 43
S R Waugh not out 10
Extras (b 3, lb 3, w 6) 12
Total (for 5, 50 overs) **266**

Fall of wickets: 1-90, 2-148, 3-159, 4-170,
5-248.
Did not bat: S P O'Donnell, #G C Dyer, T B A
May, B A Reid.
Bowling: Rawson 9-0-41-0; Jarvis 6-0-33-0;
Shah 7-0-31-0; Brandes 10-1-58-0; Traicos
10-0-42-2; Butchart 8-0-52-1.

AUSTRALIA WON BY 70 RUNS

ZIMBABWE

A Shah b Waugh 32
A Waller c Waugh b McDermott 38
K Curran c Waugh b May 29
A Pycroft c Dyer b McDermott 38
#D Houghton lbw b May 1
I Butchart st Dyer b Border 3
P Rawson not out 24
E Brandes not out 18
Extras (lb 5, nb 2, w 6) 13
Total (for 6, 50 overs) **196**

Fall of wickets: 1-55, 2-89, 3-92, 4-97, 5-139,
6-156.
Did not bat: M Jarvis, K Arnott, *J Traicos.
Bowling: McDermott 10-0-43-2; Reid
9-2-30-0; Waugh 4-0-9-1; O'Donnell 7-1-21-0;
May 10-1-30-2; Border 8-0-36-1; Jones 1-0-5-0;
Boon 1-0-17-0.

PAKISTAN v WEST INDIES

Hollow win for Richards

An innings of 110 by Richie Richardson steered the West Indies to a meaningless 28-run victory over Pakistan at Karachi, but they still go out of the World Cup, missing the final for the first time in the competition's history.

The West Indians made 258 for 7 – with Richardson sharing a third-wicket stand of 137 with his skipper Viv Richards, whose 67 made him the first batsman to score 1,000 World Cup runs. The Pakistanis, already through to the semi-finals, began slowly and, despite 70 from Rameez Raja, finished on 230 for 9.

KARACHI SCOREBOARD

WEST INDIES

D Haynes c Imran b Mudassar	25
P Simmons b Akram	6
R Richardson c Qadir b Imran	110
*I V A Richards b Akram	67
G Logie c Mudassar b Imran	12
R Harper b Akram	2
C Hooper not out	5
W Benjamin c Mudassar b Imran	0
#J Dujon not out	1
Extras (b 3, lb 10, nb 1, w 16)	30
Total (for 7, 50 overs	258

Fall of wickets: 1-19, 2-84, 3-221, 4-242, 5-248, 6-225, 7-255.
Did not bat: C Walsh, P Patterson.
Bowling: Imran 9-0-57-3; Akram 10-0-45-3; Qadir 10-1-29-0; Mudassar 10-0-47-1; Jaffer 6-0-37-0; Malik 5-0-30-0.

WEST INDIES WON BY 28 RUNS

PAKISTAN

Mudasar Nazar b Harper	40
Rameez Raja c Hooper b Patterson	70
Salim Malik c Richards b Walsh	23
Javed Miandad b Benjamin	38
Ijaz Ahmed b Benjamin	6
*Imran Khan c Harper b Walsh	8
#Salim Yousuf b Patterson	7
Wasim Akram lbw b Patterson	0
Abdul Qadir not out	8
Shoalb Mohammad b Benjamin	0
Salim Jaffer not out	8
Extras (b 4, lb 6, nb 2, w 10)	22
Total (9 wkts, 50 overs	230

Fall of wickets: 1-78, 2-128, 3-147, 4-167, 5-186, 6-202, 7-202, 8-208, 9-208.
Bowling: Patterson 10-1-34-3; Walsh 10-1-34-2; Benjamin 10-0-69-3; Harper 10-0-38-1; Richards 10-0-45-0.

INDIA v NEW ZEALAND

India top Group A

India guaranteed a World Cup semi-final place in Bombay on Thursday, following the co-hosts group victory over New Zealand at Nagpur on Saturday. India's nine-wicket win put them on top of Group A on scoring rate leaving Australia to face Pakistan on Wednesday in the other semi-final.

The scoreboard shows that New Zealand's last three overs only reaped 15 runs.

NAGPUR SCOREBOARD

NEW ZEALAND

J G Wright run out	35
P A Horne b Prabhakar	18
M D Crowe c Pandit b Azaruddin	21
K R Rutherford b Sharma	26
*J J Crowe b Maninder	24
D N Patel c Kapil Dev b Shastri	40
M C Snedden run out	23
#D S Smith b Sharma	0
E J Chatfield b Sharma	0
W K Watson not out	12
Extras (lb 14, nb 1, w 7)	22
Total (9 wkts, 50 overs)	**221**

Fall of wickets: 1-46, 2-84, 3-90, 4-122, 5-181, 6-182, 7-182, 8-182, 9-221.
Did not bat: D Morrison.
Bowling: Kapil Dev 6-0-24-0; Prabhakar 7-0-23-1; Sharma 10-2-51-3; Azaruddin 7-0-26-1; Maninder 10-0-51-1; Shastri 10-1-32-1.

INDIA

K Srikkanth c Rutherford b Watson	75
S Gavaskar not out	103
M Azharuddin not out	41
Extras (lb 1, nb 2, w 2)	5
Total (1 wkt, 32.1 overs)	**224**

Fall of wickets: 1-135
Did not bat: N S Sidhu, D B Vengaskar, *Kapil Dev, R J Shastri, #C S Pandit, M Prabhakar, C Sharma and Maninder Singh.
Bowling: Morrison 10-0-69-0; Chatfield 4.1-1-39-0; Snedden 4-0-29-0; Watson 10-0-50-1; Patel 4-0-35-0.
Umpires: H D Bird and D R Shepherd.

INDIA WON BY 9 WICKETS

Dickie Bird signals a six at Nagpur.

Sunil Gavasker on his way to his century at Nagpur.

Final Group Tables

GROUP A

	P	W	L	R/r	Pts
India	6	5	1	5.41	20
Australia	6	5	1	5.19	20
New Zealand	6	2	4	4.91	8
Zimbabwe	6	0	6	3.76	0

GROUP B

	P	W	L	R/r	Pts
Pakistan	6	5	1	5.01	20
England	6	4	2	5.12	16
West Indies	6	3	3	5.16	12
Sri Lanka	6	0	6	4.04	0

DATELINE BOMBAY, 2 /11 /87, MARTIN JOHNSON REPORTS . . .

England cast in gatecrasher's role

Connoisseurs of the commentator's gaffe can count themselves distinctly unfortunate that they're getting BBC voice-overs at home instead of the Indian original. There's enough material here to fill an Encyclopaedia Britannia-sized "Colemanballs".

There was, admittedly, a bit of bad luck attached to one observation shortly after India clinched the World Cup semi-final they wanted (home to England as opposed to away to Pakistan). "There can only be one man-of-the-match," pronounced the local equivalent of Ray Illingworth. Whereupon Sunil Gavaskar and Chetan Sharma both walked up to collect their joint award. The escape-line, however, was not brilliant. "And there they are . . . the men-of-the-match."

A little earlier, though, with India a couple of deliveries away from victory, our man came out with something rather more relevant to England – or to be more exact, to local expectations of England's future prospects. "This win," he intoned, "guarantees an all host-country final." Pause for thought. "Or at least, we hope so."

Ever since the World Cup venue was decided, the sub-continent has been hoping – understandably – for an India-Pakistan final, but what the commentator's Freudian slip revealed was that hope has now given way to expectation. And such high expectation, that the consequences of an England-Australian final are simply too awful to contemplate in a poverty-stricken land in which cricket is far and away the major form of escapism.

The odds are that there will indeed be an India-Pakistan final, but of the two semi-final matches, in Lahore on Wednesday and Bombay on Thursday, England would appear to have the better chance of spoiling the party.

Quite apart from the advantage of playing in claustrophobic Bombay, where the spectators are close enough for an England boundary fielder to be nigh on unmissable for all but the novice orange-thrower, India have a greater capacity for brilliance than England. Nonetheless, whatever the sport, flair has far from a 100 per cent success rate over efficiency.

England do, however, have a major worry before Thursday's game. Neil Foster, who injured his right knee in the second group match against Pakistan, and as a consequence has bowled variably since, is still not fully fit, and was an absentee at net practise yesterday.

What he needs is rest, but as Mike Gatting pointed out, there isn't much time for that now. Foster will be expected to bowl flat-out during Wednesday's full-scale session, otherwise the risk of his breaking down during the match will be deemed too great.

If Foster doesn't make it, England will almost certainly recall Derek Pringle, who is – according to Gatting – "bowling very well" in the nets. Unfortunately this sort of form has proved elusive out in the middle, although in fairness to Pringle his shortcomings have certainly been magnified by an absence of luck.

England won't practise every day before the match ("In this heat we'd be knackered," said Gatting), neither will they be cramming in too much swotting before their biggest examination to date. They know India's individual strengths and weaknesses pretty well, with the exception of Navjot Sidhu, who, as a former strokeless wonder turned crash-bang-wallop merchant, has undergone a Glenn Turner-like metamorphosis and has scored four eye-catching half-centuries in five World Cup innings. "All I've seen him do is charge down the wicket to the spinners and launch them over the top," said Gatting, who has never been one to over compli-cate matters.

England are also familiar (and happy) with the choice of umpires for Bombay, the Australian Tony Crafter and the New Zealander Steve Woodward, while the two English umpires are both officiating in the Lah-ore semi-final. For Dickie Bird at least, an England defeat in Bombay would almost certainly bring with it the consolation prize of being involved in the final.

DATELINE, 3/11/87, FROM OUR CORRESPONDENT ...

English
Umpires appeal to Australians

Australia feel their hopes of victory over Pakistan in tomorrow's World Cup semi-final in Lahore have improved with the news that English umpires Dickie Bird and David Shepherd will be in control.

Having been on the receiving end of what they consider to have been some dubious decisions on the sub-continent over the years, the Australians have taken new heart after the appointment of Bird and Shepherd.

"We are absolutely delighted two such high-quality umpires have been appointed to control a game of this importance," said the team manager yesterday. "We can now look forward to a contest where at the end of the day the better team will have won."

The Australian team which toured India last year found it impossible to believe that for their three Tests and six one-day internationals, a total of 18 different umpires were used. The Australian Cricket Board have no more than seven umpires on their representative panel.

With the Gaddafi Stadium crowd tomorrow sure to be hostile to the Australian team, the appointment of Bird and Shepherd may go a long way to soothing any ill-feeling between the teams which might have occurred if local umpires had been appointed.

An additional bonus for the Australians may be the absence of one of Pakistan's key players, the all-rounder Wasim Akram. Akram, who recently signed for Lancashire, fractured a small bone in his foot while batting against the West Indies in his side's final group match in Karachi, and his absence would represent a serious blow to the World Cup favourites.

Powerful though their batting line-up is, Pakistan's major strength in the competition so far has been the ability of their bowlers not only to contain, but also to take wickets at crucial stages – and in the captain Imran Khan, Abdul Qadir and Akram, they possess the most penetrative attack in the competition.

However, Imran is already on record as saying he is not satisfied with his team's fielding. "We have depth in both our batting and bowling but my biggest worry has been the fielding. The West Indies won the first two World Cups largely through their brilliant fielding, so to a lesser extent did India in 1983, and it will not be different for any side hoping to win this time."

Australia's prospects of springing an upset rest largely with their batsmen, as they do not appear to have the bowling depth to defend anything other than an above-par total.

Openers Geoff Marsh and David Boon are both in excellent form, as is Dean Jones, but they must be worried about the poor form, so far, of skipper Allan Border.

Meanwhile, England's Allan Lamb is considering offers from Western Province and Orange Free State, in his native South Africa, to play Currie Cup cricket. He will make his mind up after the World Cup.

DATELINE BOMBAY 4 /11 /87, MARTIN JOHNSON REPORTS . . .

England's iron amid the fireworks

When two sides of roughly equal ability meet in a one-day international, the accepted pre-match platitude is "XI against XI, and who does it on the day". This, however, will not apply in Bombay tomorrow, where England's XI will have to do it on the day against India's 50,000 and XI.

Within 24 hours of India securing a home semi-final last Saturday, there wasn't a spare firecracker to be had in Bombay, and by nine o'clock tomorrow morning there will be enough gunpowder inside the Wankhede Stadium to have made Exhibit A in the case against Guy Fawkes look like a pinch of snuff. The object of the exercise, one need hardly add, is to make England feel anything but at home on 5 November.

While England profess themselves to be unconcerned about the prospect of such a hostile environment, they have at least been thorough in preparing for it. Running between the wickets, for instance, creates special problems when the eardrums are being subjected to the decibel equivalent of half a dozen pneumatic drills, and contingency plans to cope have stopped only just short of a crash course in racecourse tic-tac.

There is, however, a school of thought that the crowd (you couldn't get near the stadium for cricket queues yesterday) is not guaranteed to work in India's favour. We saw it in Sharjah with both India and Pakistan. Failure provokes, if anything, an even more volatile reaction, and if things start going England's way, Kapil Dev is far more likely than Mike Gatting to have a mango explode on his head.

At the moment, anyway, it is probably true to say that England have been scouring the local papers more to check the weather than the local fruit and veg prices. It is horribly hot and humid in Bombay at the moment (35C yesterday) and in a bowl-like structure like the Wankhede it will alternate throughout the day between a sauna and an incinerator.

The sub-continent has already achieved the near impossible in reducing the England captain by 12lbs (at this rate he will have to be flown home and placed on a cheese and Branston drip) and the busiest members of the England squad tomorrow will be the 13th and 14th men, ferrying out salt tablets and bottled water to dehydrated players.

At this stage, with Paul Jarvis earmarked for the 12th man's shady seat, these duties seem likely to be shared by Chris Broad and either Neil Foster or Derek Pringle. Foster was scheduled to have a final fitness test on his injured knee today, but he was a lot happier about his prospects during yesterday's net practice.

Gatting, originally critical of the five-day gap between England's final group match and the semi-final, has now altered his opinion – not only because anything shorter would rule Foster out, but also because it has given his players extra time to acclimatise. Mostly they have played in dry heat (Peshawar has been the coolest) but Bombay's humidity has made it comfortably (or, to be more precise, uncomfortably) the most draining venue so far.

England's last remaining worry is the pitch, and what to do if they win the toss. As far as the heat goes it seems to be more comfortable fielding in the afternoon, and judging by the way the groundsman has had to take the Polyfilla to a series of little holes, the pitch's lasting properties may also be questionable.

On the other hand, the ball traditionally swings around for the first hour or two in Bombay and any moisture that may be there at 9 am will long since have been sucked out by the sun come lunch-time. One or two players think it might be a good toss to lose, but Gatting, I am sure, is planning an insertion if he wins it.

The result, though, may ultimately turn on, well, just that. Turn. Not the least refreshing aspect of this tournament has been the success of the spinners, and in Maninder Singh and Ravi Shastri on the one hand and John Emburey and Eddie Hemmings on the other, this – with apologies to Eddie – is a slow bowlers' heavyweight contest.

The World Cup pitches have generally been so slow and flat that batsmen have had to come out and hit the spinners rather than allow the ball to do the work. By contrast, the medium pacer cannot afford the slightest error in line. Even pitching middle and off, he is liable to be whipped away through mid-wicket.

Maninder and Shastri will use flight, subtle variations of pace, and rely on temptation. Emburey and Hemmings will spear it in flat at the pads to 6-3 legside fields, and rely on frustration. Both types of bowling, if accurate, force batsmen into calculated risks – and it was Hemmings who virtually clinched England's semi-final place when Viv Richards ran away to leg and attempted to cut him off the stumps.

Against anyone else India might also be tempted to play their leg-spinner, Sivaramakrishan, but the presence of Gatting – who slaughtered him on David Gower's '84-85 tour – would seem to make that an unacceptable gamble.

India must be regarded as favourites, not only because it's Bombay but also because they are such a dangerous batting side. It was a long time before they took their L-plates off in this type of cricket, and in the first ever World Cut meeting between the sides – at Lord's in 1975 – they appeared to be under the impression that it was a timeless Test. Chasing 334, they managed the not inconsiderable feat of batting through 60 overs for 132 and 3 and Sunil Gavaskar ended up on 36 not out.

Times, though, have changed, and it was Gavaskar's brilliant century against New Zealand that secured India home advantage in the semi-final. If England can win here, against the World Cup holders, it will be a better achievement than any of their four one-day tournament victories in the past 10 months.

DATELINE BOMBAY 4 /11 /87, MARTIN JOHNSON REPORTS . . .

Gooch practises art of perfection

England's anchor man is compiling runs again, but he would prefer to compose them.

It was nice of the hotel management to pipe a recording of England's World Series victory in Australia through the TV video channel last night, but if England are to win international cricket's premier one-day tournament much may depend on a player for whom the past 12 months have represented a personal video nasty.

Graham Gooch is, by his own admission, still not the player he was a couple of years ago – but after his century in the MCC Bi-centennial at Lord's and two consecutive man-of-the-match awards in this World Cup, he is again beginning to doff his helmet to acknowledge the applause rather than to apply a puzzled scratch to the top of his head.

By an ordinary player's standards, Gooch has had a perfectly acceptable past couple of years. He is, however, a far from ordinary player, and by the standards he sets for himself, it's been a little like a Ferrari running on two-stroke, or a Derby winner pulling a milk float.

"I'm a lot happier now," said Gooch, "but I really don't feel I've played particularly well for the past couple of years. I've still made runs, but not in the way I'd have liked, and without being big-headed, I'm not satisfied with simply being average."

Gooch waits to open the England innings on the balcony at Gujranwala.

So far in this World Cup Gooch has played in a solid, dependable way, with just the occasional flash of genius, but invaluable though his anchor role has been – particularly in the crucial second match against the West Indies – it's not been through either choice or instruction.

"Quite honestly, I'm still not the player I once was. I'm compiling an innings, rather than playing by instinct, and the runs aren't coming in the same way. So much of this game is down to confidence, and I've even wondered at times whether old age has crept up and pinched the old skills forever.

"It's a funny thing being out of form. Instead of being natural you tend to think about each ball more technically – more so than is probably good for you. It's a bit like golf. Whack the first couple of drives down the middle and you're away. A couple of duffs, on the other hand, and you're fiddling around with the grip, stance, you name it, and nothing feels quite right.

Had it not been for last summer's problems, which culminated in his handing back the Essex captaincy to Keith Fletcher, Gooch might not have made himself available for the World Cup, but after missing Australia, he felt he owed it to himself "to prove I could still do it."

Gooch, though, remains a reluctant tourist nowadays. Not because of the cricket side of it – "I love playing for England, home and away. But last winter, I wanted to be at home when my twins were born, and quite honestly your perspective changes when you've a young family. This year's complete package I frankly find horrendous, and I really can't see why the New Zealand leg could not have been put off.

"People might have wondered why I chose to spend last winter at home in the cold with three screaming kids rather than on a beach sipping a can of Toohey's, but the more trips you've done the more your values change. In my case I feel I can never replace the years watching the kids grow up, but mental fatigue also comes into it, as it has with David Gower. The authorities will either have to rethink tours, or accept more and more players opting out. It's unlikely I'll be doing much more touring."

At the moment, though, Gooch's thoughts are geared to England's World Cup effort. He missed the 1983 tournament because of his three-year South African "rebel" tour ban, but as the only member of the 14-man squad to have experienced playing in a World Cup final – in 1979 – he'd dearly like another taste.

"I've been telling the lads that occasions like that are the reason you're in the game in the first place, and I think we have a more than decent chance of getting there this time. India are a fine side, no two ways about it, but while we've not been very spectacular so far we've operated well as a team and our wins have all been solid and professional.

"As for the two defeats, we were in winning positions both times, but Pakistan held it together much better when the pressure was on. We collapsed badly in the first game against them, but you have to give credit to Wasim Akram, who bowled magnificently at the death."

1st SEMI-FINAL PAKISTAN v AUSTRALIA
Aussies take Waugh path to final party

If it had not been for the risk of sunburn, not to mention a fine for infringing the local bye-laws, you would have put your shirt on Pakistan in Lahore yesterday. Instead, it turned out to be one of those "cricket is a funny game" days, and it was Australia – the side that this time last year could not beat a drum – who advanced, and convincingly at that, into Sunday's World Cup final.

It was doubly ungracious of the Australians, who have not only gate-crashed the sub-continent's non-surprise party (all India v Pakistan tickets back to the printers, please) but also kyboshed the second leg of Imran Khan's retirement double. Having already led Pakistan to their first-ever Test series victory in England, Imran badly wanted the World Cup to go with it, but in the end, his team could not handle the pressure of carrying not so much the hopes but the demands of an entire nation.

There could scarcely have been a bigger contrast between 9 am at the Gaddafi Stadium, and 5 pm. At the start of the match, it was a bit like an open-air Beatles concert from the Sixties, a cacophony of noise augmented by the screams from Imran's teenage girl fan club packed inside the ladies section. By the end, you could almost have heard the sound of the nib scratching Australia's name on to the winners' cheque.

Initially, it seemed, the atmosphere would get to Australia more than Pakistan. Geoff Marsh, surrounded by more people than can ever wander through Wandering – his native Western Australian sheep town – in an entire year, could scarcely pick his bat up for nerves. But he eventually recovered, and ultimately it was temperament as much as ability that got Australia through.

They had some luck as well. Pakistan dropped four catches and the ground fielding (Imran's big worry) also let them down. Australia's frantic running between the wickets cost them three run-outs, but it also meant that they never completely surrendered the initiative when Qadir and Tauseef were stemming the tide in mid-innings.

On top of that, Javed Miandad had to keep wicket for more than half the innings after Salim Yousuf had been hit in the mouth by a ball from Tauseef. Whether this qualified as a handicap or a bonus is hard to say, but the real blow for Pakistan was the dreadful bowling of Saleem Jaffer.

Imran may have given him the new ball because of Wasim Akram's foot injury (Akram was, after all, able to play after discovering that he had only chipped rather than fractured a bone), but Jaffer had been so awful early on that there is no explanation at all as to why Imran should have entrusted him with the 50th over.

Steve Waugh plundered 18 from it (the eventual margin victory) and while a superb second spell from Imran prevented Australia from scoring the 300 they at one time looked capable of, that final over represented a vast psychological sing.

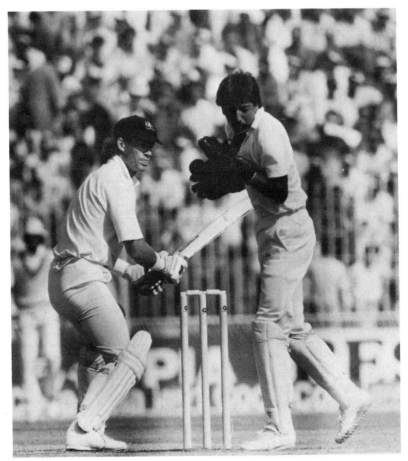

Salim Yousuf is hit by a ball from Tauseef.

Jones signals that Yousuf has been hit in the mouth.

Yousuf is helped off, his match over.

Substitute "keeper" Miandad stumps David Boon.

Pakistan, one felt, were still marginal favourites to make the 268 they needed even on a pitch that was slow and variable in bounce. However, while we were well aware of Australia's batting and fielding strength it was not clear until yesterday how quickly their bowling has matured.

This applies particularly to Craig McDermott. Last winter, McDermott had almost as much trouble with his temper as his aim, but he has now acquired the twin arts of pitching the ball up into the block-hole and not allowing the odd loose one to blow every mental fuse in his head. Simon O'Donnell also proved difficult to slog, largely by using the waist-high full-toss theory.

Pakistan put themselves under immediate pressure when Ramiz Raja was run out off the third ball of the innings and then losing two more batsmen (including the in-form Salim Malik) before the shine had even gone off the ball.

It fell to Imran and Javed to effect the repairs but the size of the damage inevitably made a mess of the asking rate. They put on 112, but at not much above four an over, and the requirement was well above seven when Imran edged a catch behind.

Craig McDonald runs out Ramiz Raja on only the third ball of the innings.

The Ladies' enclosure at Lahore.

Akram smashed a couple of sixes but Javed had been so consumed by his anchor role that *rigor mortis* had set in when it was finally time to cut loose. The chanting finally stopped when Bruce Reid defeated Javed's desperate slog, and as McDermott mopped up the tail, you would not have known whether it was a World Cup semi-final or a meeting of the Lahore Noise Abatement Society.

General Zia put on a brave smile at the awards ceremony, but the Pakistan players were down in the mouth. What they lost in rupees yesterday is difficult to calculate, but it probably makes the Wall Street crash equate to a small boy's sweet-shop raid on his piggy bank.

LAHORE SCOREBOARD

AUSTRALIA

G R Marsh run out 31
D C Boon st Miandad b Malik 65
D M Jones b Tauseef 38
*A R Border run out 18
M R J Veletta b Imran 48
S R Waugh not out 32
S P O'Donnell run out 0
#G C Dyer b Imran 0
C J McDermott b Imran 1
T B A May not out 0
Extras (b 1, lb 19, w 13, nb 1) 34
Total (for 8, 50 overs) 267

Fall of wicket: 1-73, 2-155, 3-155, 4-215, 5-236, 6-236, 7-241, 8-249.
Did not bat: B A Reid.
Bowling: Imran 10-1-36-3; Jaffer 6-0-57-0; Akram 10-0-54-0; Qadir 10-0-39-0; Tauseef 10-1-39-1; Malik 4-0-22-1.

PAKISTAN

Ramiz Raja run out 1
Mansoor Akhtar b McDermott 9
Salim Malik c McDermott b Waugh 25
Javed Miandad b Reid 70
*Imran Khan c Dyer b Border 58
Wasim Akram b McDermott 20
Ijaz Ahmed c Jones b Reid 8
#Salim Yousuf c Dyer b McDermott 21
Abdul Qadir not out 20
Saleem Jaffer c Dyer b McDermott 0
Tauseef Ahmed c Dyer b McDermott 1
Extras (lb 6, w 10) 16
Total (49 overs) 249

Fall of wicket: 1-2, 2-37, 3-38, 4-150, 5-177, 6-192, 7-212, 8-236, 9-247.
Bowling: McDermott 10-0-44-5; Reid 10-2-41-2; Waugh 9-1-51-1; O'Donnell 10-0-45-0; May 6-0-36-0; Border 4-0-26-1.

AUSTRALIA WON BY 18 RUNS

2nd SEMI-FINAL INDIA v ENGLAND

First-class Gooch books final ticket

There were umpteen million candidates for owner of the longest face in India last night, but the winner was probably a Calcutta ticket tout. It will be a buyer's market at Eden Gardens, on Sunday, for the World Cup final no one on the sub-continent wanted, England versus Australia.

The widest smile, on the other hand, belonged to Mike Gatting, and it was also quite a day for collectors of cricketing memorabilia. There it was, rarer than a Bradman autograph, but I kid you not. A Goochie grin.

Gooch, who rarely goes public with any fluctuation of mood, was as transparently chuffed about yesterday as any single day in his cricketing career. And with good reason. He has batted outstandingly all through the tournament, but this one was nonpareil in terms of both quality and importance.

The pitch was anything but ideal ("dreadful" was Gatting's summing-up) for a one-day match – slow, low, and turning quite sharply on occasions. Made to measure, in fact, for India's attack, but while virtually everyone else struggled, Gooch's command was so total that he made it look like an Oval shirt-front.

There was a sharp difference of opinion among the four England selectors about what to do if they won the toss: bat (Gooch and Emburey) or bowl (Gatting and Stewart). In the end, though, Kapil got the choice, but despite an atmosphere that turned the Wankhede into a giant Turkish bath, there was no undue new-ball movement all day.

The key to England's innings was the Indian spinners, and Gooch formulated his game-plan against them after the first ball he received from Maninder, which turned at right-angles and crept through at worm-height. From that moment, he fed the lap – the pro's term for the sweep-cum-paddle shot – into his computer, and thanks to the fact that the opposition sportingly omitted to set a field to combat it, was never obliged to re-program.

Within 64 deliveries, Gooch had made 50 out of a total of 67 in 19 overs, and his fifth one-day international century eventually came off 120 balls out of a 36-over total of 157. What was so impressive about his scoring rate was the way he did it with scarcely a reference to his favourite stroke. On this pitch, with the ball hobbling through on crutches, the front-foot drive carried an unacceptable risk.

Mike Gatting feels the heat as he returns to the pavilion after being bowled for 56.

Gooch's major ally, in a third-wicket partnership of 117 in 19 overs, was Gatting, who somehow managed a half-century that was almost as gruesome as his eventual death – sweeping a ball from Maninder on to his leg stump. It was, though, undeniably invaluable, not least for the amount of time he spent scuffing up the pitch (accidentally I'm sure) with a pair of rarely-worn spikes. After the skipper has charged down for a quick single, it's the equivalent of four days' wear in a Test match.

By contrast, Gooch's hairiest moment (apart from the time he was nearly run out having to make a major detour around the on-rushing Gatting) was when he top-edged a difficult leg-side chance to Srikkanth.

Kiran More, the Indian Keeper, during England's innings at Bombay.

That went down, which pleased the crowd even less than a hapless exhibition of fielding out on the mid-wicket boundary, where Pandit received such a pelting that he was eventually knee-deep in cardboard sunhats. As we saw in Lahore, passionate crowds don't always mean forgiving ones.

With Allan Lamb supervising the late slog, England eventually posted a total so well above par for the conditions ("I'd have taken 230 gladly at the start," said Gatting) that only a poor bowling performance, one felt, could have denied them.

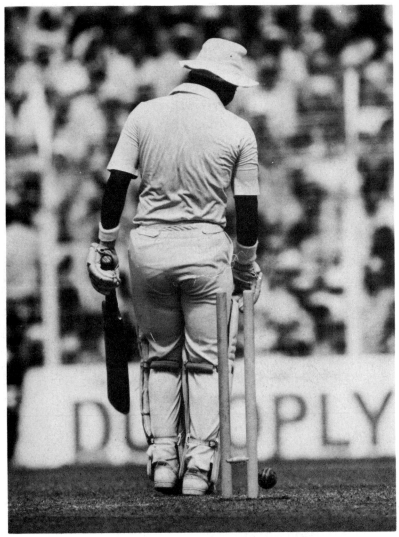

Gavaskar's bowled.

They also had the bonus of not having to bowl at one of the world's best batsmen, Dilip Vengsarkar. He was out with a nasty bout of food poisoning, traced back to a meal after India's final group-match against New Zealand, and if England are planning any "thank you for your support" telegrams, there should be one on its way to a fishmonger in Nagpur.

England could scarcely have made a better start, with Phillip DeFreitas bowling Sunil Gavaskar off his pads in the third over of the

DeFreitas celebrates the breakthrough.

innings. That vital early wicket undoubtedly had a major bearing on the outcome, which in turn spared Gavaskar the ticklish problem of whether or not to play in the final. On England's last tour here, three years ago, Gavaskar had to be given a police escort off the ground in Calcutta, where they have little love for natives of Bombay, and he's since stuck by his vow never to play there again.

Bill Athey and Neil Foster celebrate their roles in the dismissal of Sidhu.

However, England managed to make things much harder for themselves by not consistently adhering to the very thing they're supposed to be better at than any other side out here, length and line. Neil Foster, despite picking up three wickets, was ultimately flattered by his figures.

The game hinged, and eventually turned, on Eddie Hemmings, whose first three overs had gone for 27, and whose return coincided with a furious (and curious) bout of slogging from Kapil Dev. With India quietly picking off the runs at a disturbing rate, Kapil arrived in mid-innings apparently under the impression that the game had to be won in the next ten minutes, and enjoyed some outrageous luck in scoring 30 off 22 balls.

He'd just hoiked Hemmings for four to mid-wicket when the spinner requested Gatting to drop back to the boundary. Next ball Kapil lofted a catch straight to him. As logical thought processes go, it was almost as mind-boggling as the way India then set about the far from impossible task of making 56 from the final 10 overs with five wickets in hand.

Once Azharuddin had gone, after a well-placed innings, the only sensible plan for the rest was to give the strike to the dangerous Ravi Shastri. Instead, they all got out thrashing away at everything, and when Shastri was last out top-edging Hemmings, India had lost those last five wickets in 33 balls for 20 runs, and the match by the deceptive margin of 35 runs.

After the cracking build-up of tension, it all fell oddly flat – although flat is hardly the word to describe the England players last night, Gooch in particular. There is certain to be a new name on the World Cup on Sunday, and with Gooch in this sort of mood – this was his third consecutive man-of-the-match award – the odds on it being England's look encouragingly short.

BOMBAY SCOREBOARD

ENGLAND

G A Gooch c Srikkanth b Maninder 115
R T Robinson st More b Maninder 13
C W J Athey c More b Sharma 4
*M W Gatting b Maninder 56
A J Lamb not out 32
J E Emburey lbw b Kapil Dev 6
P A J DeFreitas b Kapil Dev 7
#P R Downton not out 1
Extras (b 1, lb 18, nb 1) 20
Total (for 6, 50 overs) 254

Fall of wickets: 1-40, 2-79, 3-196, 4-203, 5-219, 6-231.
Did not bat: N A Foster, G C Small, E E Hemmings.
Bowling: Kapil Dev 10-1-38-2; Prabhakar 9-1-40-0; Maninder 10-0-54-3; Sharma 9-0-41-1; Shastri 10-0-49-0; Azharuddin 2-0-13-0.

INDIA

K Srikkanth b Foster 31
S M Gavaskar b DeFreitas 4
N Sidhu c Athey b Foster 22
M Azharuddin lbw b Hemmings 64
C S Pandit lbw b Foster 24
*Kapil Dev c Gatting b Hemmings 30
R J Shastri c Downton b Hemmings 21
#K S More c and b Emburey 0
M Prabhakar c Downton b Small 4
C Sharma c Lamb b Hemmings 0
Maninder Singh not out 0
Extras (b 1, lb 9, w 6, nb 3) 19
Total (45.3 overs) 219

Fall of wickets: 1-7, 2-58, 3-73, 4-121, 5-168, 6-204, 7-205, 8-218, 9-219.
Bowling: DeFreitas 7-0-37-1; Small 6-0-22-1; Emburey 10-1-35-1; Foster 10-0-47-3; Hemmings 9.3-1-52-4; Gooch 3-0-16-0.

ENGLAND WON BY 35 RUNS

A nine-year-old girl was stabbed and 28 people injured when cricket supporters battled with each other after England's win in Bombay. The Press Trust of India reported that 21 were hurt in Bombay when groups using stones and soda-water bottles clashed, and in Ahmedabad as well as the stabbing six others, including three women, were hurt.

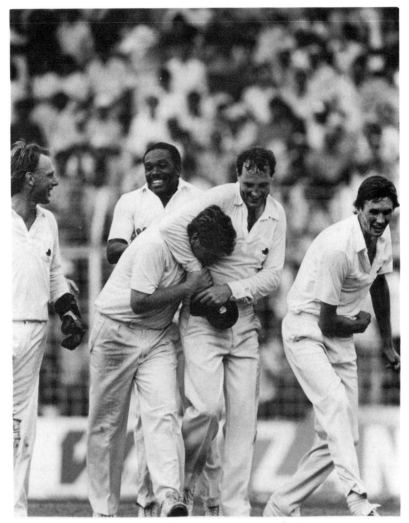

The England players celebrate victory.

Kapil's tactics are a hard slog

Kapil Dev's captaincy has never been his strongest point, and during the World Cup his failure to read the game has more than once cost India dear. His first bowling change after England began their innings this morning was a major turning point, as was the wasteful slog which cost him his wicket.

It suited England to bat first, but Graham Gooch and Tim Robinson were understandably cautious about the pitch. There was movement off the seam, and the ball swung in the humidity. Kapil himself and Manoj Prabhakar each bowled five very tight overs, and the England openers scored only 20 runs in the first 10 overs.

At that point India were in charge, and Kapil should have done everything to put them even further behind the clock in the hope that the batsmen would, in their frustration, get themselves out. He should have kept himself and Prabhakar on for at least two more overs each. As it was he brought on Maninder Singh, eight runs came off the 11th over and the pressure disappeared.

On the type of pitches found in Bangalore, Madras or Delhi, it would have made good sense to bring Maninder on after only 10 overs but with the ball not coming through on to the bat, Kapil and Prabhakar quickly built up a strong position. By throwing the ball to Maninder, Kapil surrendered the initiative, and in no time England were scoring at an overall average of nearly four an over.

Later, when Kapil was batting, it looked as if India would win the match with some ease. He then lost his head, determined to hit everything out of sight. If he could have throttled back, India would probably have won with something to spare.

As it was, he slogged needlessly, was caught at deep mid-wicket, and from that moment India were swept along on a fierce tide of panic, and with clinical and professional precision England took full advantage of it. Kapil has much to answer for.

THE INDEPENDENT

World Cup final: Gatting may welcome back Broad who shares Gooch's capacity for arousing Aussie apprehension

A Scottish psychiatrist recently came up with the statistic that World Cups coincide with a drop in the suicide rate. This may soon be subject to re-appraisal, because the urge to jump under a bus is pretty strong on the sub-continent at the moment.

The latest "official" prefix in this competition has been jointly claimed by England and Australia who, by ungraciously conspiring to contest tomorrow's final in Calcutta, have become official party-poopers to the World Cup.

What makes it all the more galling is that it comes at a time when plans are afoot to put the two founder members firmly in their place at the International Cricket Conference's latest political punch-up on Monday.

One immediate repercussion of the two semi-final results has been the cancellation of the "World Cup winners versus the Rest" match in Calcutta on Tuesday, partly because recent events have rendered the wretched game even more irrelevant than it was in the first place, and more pertinently because potential champions Australia have already made it clear that they will be unavailable on that date for anything other than a few beers on the Qantas flight home. It has to be said that this news has not exactly had England reaching for the Kleenex.

The shock of failure has brought with it contrasting reactions from both the public and the Press. Captain Mike Gatting has had his hand pumped with genuine warmth, but he has also (as have several other England players) received the odd abusive telephone call. The one he got on Thursday night was a little gem. "Mike Gatting?" "Speaking." "You should have lost. Javed Miandad should have punched you in the face when he had the chance in Rawalpindi. He's a gentleman, that Javed."

Very nice. As for the Press, some newspapers have put it down to bad luck ("The invisible hand of Allah"), and others are out for blood.

Before the semi-final, the *Pakistan Times* wanted Imran to be appointed King. After it, they said: "After one of the most shocking upsets in World Cup history, Imran is now history himself." Hero to villain in 100 overs. Not much different to the English Press really.

Mike Gatting has led from the front.

And so to Sunday's hero. Mike Gatting or Allan Border? The bookies go for Gatting, and while there is not too much difference between the sides in terms of batting (England by a nose, probably) and fielding (Australia, but it's close), England do appear to have a clear edge in the bowling stakes.

As it happens, England have yet to produce their first entirely satisfactory bowling performance. John Emburey and Phillip DeFreitas have been the most consistent, but there is still too much loose stuff for comfort. If England had bowled anything like in Bombay, India would not have smelled 200.

They do, though, appear to have the knack of taking wickets at vital times, none more so than Neil Foster. A stern self-critic, one of the recurring memories of this World Cup will be Foster beating himself angrily on the rump after a couple of lousy deliveries, then producing something unplayable next ball.

Australia, on the other hand, have been making the best of a pretty ordinary lot. Bruce Reid was struggling until the semi-final, and while Craig McDermott and Steve Waugh appear to be bowling with good control, Australia's winter hero, Peter Taylor, can no longer hold down a place, and England are unlikely to lose much sleep over the medium pace of Simon O'Donnell and the off-spin of Tim May.

England will consider only one change to the side they've put out in the last four matches, whether to recall Chris Broad in place of Tim Robinson who, apart from his half-century against Sri Lanka in Pune, has not looked entirely convincing.

The International Cricketer of the Year has, in this competition, become the International Drinks Waiter of the Year, and is more than a little miffed about it. However, Broad is ideally equipped to deal with Reid's inslanting deliveries to the left-hander – as he demonstrated so memorably last winter – and the mere fact that the Australians will probably go pale at the mere sight of him may be sufficient to earn him a recall.

By the same token, the Australians might even have considered leaving out David Boon had Graham Dilley been here. Dilley only had to say good morning to him in Australia for Boon to start walking to the pavilion, but the roly-poly Tasmanian has recovered so well from those traumas that he has been – along with Gooch – the outstanding batsman of this World Cup. He and Geoff Marsh represent the most formidable opening partnership in the competition, although their understanding between the wickets is sometimes more psychopathic than telepathic, and England's best plan might well be to bowl for the run-out.

The Australian bowlers will, of course, be apprehensive about Gooch, whose century on Thursday raised his competition aggregate to 436 runs (average 62.28) in seven matches – a World Cup record.

Gooch, who missed the 1983 tournament because of his three-year ban, has now scored 646 World Cup runs, bettered only by Viv Richards (1,013 at an average of 63.31, in 23 matches), and Gooch is also the only player to have won three consecutive World Cup man-of-the-match awards.

The two umpires for the final will be Maboob Shah from Pakistan and Ram Gupta from India. Border, with Gatting's approval, had made a special request for Dickie Bird and the Australian Tony Crafter, but it would have been asking a lot for the host nations to deny themselves even this minor representation on the big day.

DATELINE CALCUTTA, 7/11/87, HENRY BLOFELD REPORTS...

Border's men look fit to stage an exhibition

One of the surprises of the World Cup has been the form of Allan Border's Australians. Since the retirement of Greg Chappell, Dennis Lillee and Rod Marsh, Australian cricket has been in a mess.

First, there were the captaincy problems which resulted in Kim Hughes's departure. The dressing room was not a happy place and was not helped by the appointment of a full-time manager, Bob Merriman, who had none of the necessary qualifications.

Eighteen months ago Bobby Simpson took over as cricketing manager but results were still slow in materialising. Although the atmosphere in the dressing room improved there were still players who were far from being ideal team men.

The selectors at last faced this problem when they chose the side for the World Cup and the prima-donnas have all been left behind. Having visited Australia every season since 1974-5, I feel qualified to say that they have not had such a fit and determined side since Ian Chappell's captaincy a decade ago.

Players have all worked extremely hard since arriving in India, there is an excellent team spirit, Border himself is more relaxed than ever before, they have an excellent manager in Allan Crompton, surely a future chairman of the Board, and Simpson has them playing to a higher all-round level of efficiency.

Their confidence was given the boost it needed in their first match in Madras. They had one or two lucky breaks, it is true, but they beat India by one run when Steve Waugh bowled Maninder Singh off the last ball of the match. Theirs has been a team success with almost everyone playing

Allan Border (far left): a thoughtful captain.

a part, although the two most important players have been David Boon and Waugh. The only disappointment has been the form of their main off-spinner, Peter Taylor, who suddenly found himself elevated from the Sydney grade to Test cricket last December.

Boon and Geoff Marsh are admirable foils for each other at the start of the innings. While Marsh accumulates unobtrusively, apart from a lovely cover drive, Boon has become a dasher. They have shown that there is no surer way of undermining the confidence of your opponents than by having 50 on the board after 10 overs.

Boon is one of those players who loves to hit the ball hard from the moment he comes in and has become a dangerous and most exciting batsman. He is always prepared to take on any bowler.

He is not an elegant player. He is a short, chunkily-built man who wields his bat like a blunt instrument and gives the ball an almighty whack. His one problem is an exceedingly short fuse when given out and an extreme reluctance to leave the crease.

Waugh has been a key member of the side, although he should bat higher than six. He is lovely, clean stroke-maker who plays with a beautifully straight bat and has made important runs throughout the tournament, not least when he took 18 off Saleem Jaffer's last over in Wednesday's semi-final.

But his bowling has also been crucially important. At just above medium pace he has good control and the ability to move the ball off the seam. He has been a great asset in the closing or "slog" overs as the current World Cup cliché has it, for he is good at bowling straight and pitching the ball in the block hole.

Boon and Waugh are the two England have to fear the most. Their vibrant form is symptomatic of the way the whole of this Australian team are functioning and another sure sign that all is well is that they are fielding as Australian sides are traditionally expected to field. Surprisingly, Border has yet to make much of a contribution with the bat, but he is a such fine player that his best form is never more than one innings away.

World Cup Cricket '87
The Final

AUSTRALIA	ENGLAND
D.C. Boon	G.A. Gooch
G.R. Marsh	R.T. Robinson
D.M. Jones	C.W.J. Athey
C.J. McDermott	M.W. Gatting (Capt)
A. R Border (Capt)	A.J. Lamb
M.R.J. Veletta	P.R. Downtown
S.R. Waugh	J.E. Emburey
S.P. O'Donnell	P.A.J. DeFreitas
G. Dyer	N.A. Foster
T. May	G.C. Small
B.A. Reid	E.E. Hemmings

Umpires R.B. Gupta (India) M. Shah (Pakistan)

AUSTRALIA v ENGLAND

England's bowlers hand over the reins

In as much as it's possible to freeze in near 100-degree heat, the half-hour or so it took England to shake off the tension in Calcutta yesterday probably cost them the World Cup. There were other factors, but it may well be the only game in 111 years of international cricket that they effectively lost by 9.30 in the morning.

More often than not it's the batting side that feels the early pressure most, but if there was a nervous twitch about the Australian openers, it can only have been from the "beware of Pommies bearing gifts" syndrome.

Gladstone Small and Phillip DeFreitas began as though England had concocted a plan to excite the Australians out, and by the time Geoff Marsh and David Boon had worked out that it was the World Cup final and not a benefit game they were off and running with 48 off nine overs.

There was even a maiden in that, and while England recovered well enough – largely through Neil Foster and the two spinners – to make their

The Calcutta pitch is rolled.

Geoff Marsh leads Australia out to bat.

target at least negotiable, they eventually failed by seven runs to become the first team to win this competition batting second.

The fact that no fewer than 19 matches in 27 have been won batting first out here is also a revealing statistic. The pitches have merely started out dead, while they've finished in urgent need of embalmment. This one was no exception, and the only thing it did quickly was wear – to the extent that even Allan Border was getting it to turn by mid-afternoon.

Border generously conceded Australia had had the better of the conditions, and Gatting would also have batted first had he not lost his fifth consecutive toss. However, the reason that Border was sipping champagne in his own dressing room last night – instead of nipping next door as he usually has to share some of England's – had more to do with bad cricket than bad luck.

Foster, for example, ought to have bowled his 10 overs straight through instead of being taken off with figures of 1 for 16 in eight. Although a little tired, he was bowling particularly well at the time, and the fact that he is noted for having an engine that starts only reluctantly from cold was borne out when his last two went for 22.

Small made a brief but not very successful return in mid-innings, and he also gave away no-balls and wides. All told, England donated Australia another two overs with illegal deliveries, and although Graham Gooch did a fair job as sixth bowler, it was all much less forgivable than either Gat-

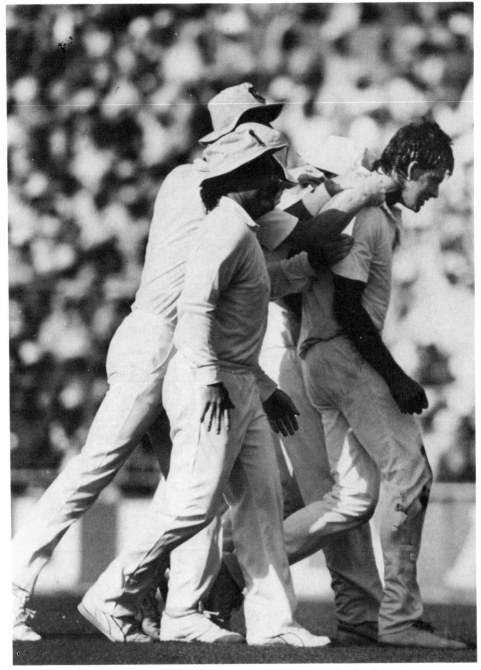

Simon O'Donnell is congratulated by team mates on his dismissal of Gooch.

Allan Lamb and Allan Border become entangled . . .

. . . and disentangled.

ting or manager Micky Stewart would have had us believe afterwards.

England had a clear advantage in bowling strength, or so we fondly imagined, and Australia should have made no more than the 230 or so that Gatting felt was around par. Once England settled Australia struggled, and the cultured Dean Jones was ultimately reduced to slogging.

Even man-of-the-match Boon got bogged down, his 75 coming off 125 balls, but Border's partnership of 73 in 12 overs with Mike Veletta gave fresh stimulus to a stagnating innings, and 79 came from the final 10 overs. The 250-plus total eventually represented a large psychological barrier.

Within four deliveries of the England innings it was even larger. The Board-Robinson discussion would certainly have taken longer than its outcome (Robinson lbw first ball to the much improved Craig McDermott) and the umpire's decision was considerably sounder, one suspects than the one made in selection.

Gooch's lbw to Simon O'Donnell was more a matter for debate, although its consequences certainly were not. Bill Athey played soundly enough to keep the score-board ticking over, but the key to England's

Bill Athey during his innings of 58.

Allan Border appeals for the run out of Bill Athey.

success here has been Gooch's ability to score rapidly and with minimal risk. When he went, the role fell to Gatting, who always scores rapidly, but with a risk factor that would produce a hang-glider's premium.

Gatting's greatest strength – the conviction that no one can bowl to him – can also be his greatest weakness. He hit the off-spinner Tim May out of the attack, but only after Steve Waugh had stepped back over the rope in taking a catch at long-on, and when he and Athey had put on 69 in 14 overs, Gatting was out – for the first time in all probability – playing the reverse sweep.

The stroke itself, especially the way Gatting plays it, is a perfectly legitimate one, whatever the views of Peter May. However, to attempt it to Border's first ball was more than a little startling. Thanks to a thickish edge (and in the opinion of some observers, a thickish head as well) the ball plopped into the wicketkeeper's gloves, and the England chairman – watching from the VIP box – very probably laid an egg.

Gatting, who had already unveiled the shot for the benefit of May (Tim, that is), is no slouch when it comes to finding peculiar ways of getting out, and England suffered another crucial setback when Athey fatally backed his legs against Bruce Reid's arm over a third run.

Lamb is down, England are almost out and Athey calls for assistance.

England needed 75 to win from the final 10 overs, four less than Australia made in that period. However, the pressures are altogether different when you're chasing, and even Allan Lamb's brisk 45 could not stop the asking rate from creeping steadily up.

Lamb eventually felt he had to slog and lost his off stump to Waugh, and while DeFreitas – using the same method to greater effect – briefly rekindled England's hopes by carting McDermott for two fours and a six in three balls, when he holed out attempting another big one off Waugh in the penultimate over, the match had gone.

As darkness closed in, Australia went on a lap of honour with the trophy, while our lads had to make do with the perfectly ludicrous sight of Peter May doing a lap, in some kind of motorised buggy, and waving a silver plate at the crowd. Disappointed though they were, the tears streaming down the losers' cheeks had nothing to do with the result.

WORLD CUP FINAL SCOREBOARD

AUSTRALIA

D C Boon c Downton b Hemmings	75
G R Marsh b Foster	24
D M Jones c Athey b Hemmings	33
C J McDermott b Gooch	14
*A R Border run out	31
M R J Veletta not out	45
S R Waugh not out	5
Extras (b 1, lb 13, w 5, nb 7)	26
Total (for 5, 50 overs)	**253**

Fall of wickets: 1-75, 2-151, 3-166, 4-168, 5-241.

Did not bat: S P O'Donnell, #G Dyer, T May, B A Reid.

Bowling: DeFreitas 6-1-34-0; Small 6-0-33-0; Foster 10-0-38-1; Hemmings 10-1-48-2; Emburey 10-0-44-0; Gooch 8-1-42-1.

Umpires(R B Gupta (India) and M Shah (Pakistan).

AUSTRALIA WON BY SEVEN RUNS

ENGLAND

G A Gooch lbw b O'Donnell	35
R T Robinson lbw b McDermott	0
C W J Athey run out	58
*M W Gatting c Dyer b Border	41
A J Lamb b Waugh	45
#P R Downton c O'Donnell b Border	9
J E Emburey run out	10
P A J DeFreitas c Reid b Waugh	17
N A Foster not out	7
G C Small not out	3
Extras (b 1, lb 14, w 2, nb 4)	21
Total (for 8, 50 overs)	**246**

Fall of wickets: 1-1, 2-66, 3-135, 4-170, 5-188, 6-218, 7-220, 8-235.

Did not bat: E E Hemmings.

Bowling: McDermott 10-1-51-1; Reid 10-0-43-0; Waugh 9-0-37-2; O'Donnell 10-1-35-1; May 4-0-27-0; Border 7-0-38-2.

DATELINE CALCUTTA, 9/11/87, MARTIN JOHNSON REPORTS . . .

Gatting reverses charges

After the game Mike Gatting the England captain, refuted criticism that his ill-fated reverse sweep to Allan Border's first delivery was a direct cause of his side's downfall.

Gatting's dismissal gave Australia a breakthrough just as their hold on the World Cup was starting to slip, but the England captain said: "Were a couple of their dismissals wise shots? Just because mine was a reverse sweep doesn't make it any different. The sooner people accept it as a legitimate one day stroke, the better.

"Perhaps as it was Allan's first ball I must take limited responsibility. But we had to keep up with the rate and make sure our score was ticking over. I don't think blame should be laid on any one department, either the batters or the bowlers." However, when further questioned by Indian journalists Gatting snapped back: "I played a reckless shot. We lost the match."

England manager Micky Stewart said: "We probably conceded 15 or 20 more runs than we would normally expect."

Allan Border, the Australian skipper, was predictably effusive. "A new era has begun in Australian cricket," he said. "We not only claimed the World Cup for the first time, but also beat two of the favourites – India and Pakistan – on our way to the final."

"This is the result of a couple of years of hard work by the team and I'm delighted for everyone. There were three wickets we wanted – Gooch, Gatting and Lamb. Once we had those wickets I thought we would win."

DATELINE CALCUTTA, 9/11/87, HENRY BLOFELD REPORTS...

Sins of Eden in the mind

It was extraordinarily moving to listen to 90,000 Indians cheering Allan Border's Australians after they had beaten England by seven runs in the heartland of Indian cricket at Eden Gardens. They stayed for more than an hour after the game.

Walking back to my hotel afterwards one was left not with the sadness of a match lost but rather with the joy of being there at all. It didn't matter who had won or lost. With the firework display lighting the neighbourhood and spontaneous applause greeting every clutch of colourful stars, even the constant blaring of car horns, the drifting dust and the sultry smog seemed like old friends.

One was left to marvel at Steve Waugh's last three overs, the joyful slogging of Phillip DeFreitas and at each piece of the jigsaw as it had fallen into place since the anticipatory walk to the grounds soon after 7 am.

It could not have mattered less that England lost for they had played a noble part. But then, as probably they must, questions and doubts followed.

Why did as experienced a cricketer as Gladstone Small forget all that he had ever been taught in the first few overs. DeFreitas also trans-

Allan Border aloft with World Cup Trophy.

gressed and Australia reached 50 before 10 overs were up. They were decisive runs.

England went in and Tim Robinson, who has played forward all his life to good-length balls decided to play back. Bill Athey apparently forgot how to push the singles, quick or slow, and think of the difference even five more runs would have made.

Most criminal of all, at least 10 full tosses were wasted by batsmen playing international cricket.

Mike Gatting's reverse sweep was a masterpiece of bad judgement; so too was that third run of Athey's. It took all of those things to go wrong and still England lost by only seven runs.

All these lapses can be explained by one word: pressure. Nerves play such an important part and on these occasions it is surely the mind that fails even the best.

On the day, human nature gave Australia a helping hand, just as surely it cheated England. It is nice to think that sometimes the occasion is too big for the man, for so often one has to suffer the man who thinks he is too big for the occasion and ultimately for the game. Eden Gardens on 8 November was, quite simply, a resounding triumph for cricket.

POST WORLD CUP

PAKISTAN TOUR: 12 November *arrive Islamabad;* **14-16** three-day match, Rawalpindi; **17** *Islamabad-Lahore;* **18** one-day international, Lahore; **19** *Lahore-Karachi;* **20** one-day international, Karachi; **21** *Karachi-Islamabad-Peshawar;* **22** one-day international Peshawar; **23** *Peshawar-Lahore;* **25-30** First Test, Lahore; **1 December** *Lahore-Sahiwal;* **2-4** three-day Sahiwal; **5** *Sahiwal-Faisalabad;* **7-12** Second Test, Faisalabad *Faisalabad-Karachi;* **16-20** Third Test, Karachi; **23** *Karachi-Heathrow 0700-1545.*

NEW ZEALAND TOUR: 13 January *depart Heathrow 15.30;* **15** *arrive Christchurch;* **18-20** three-day match v Wellington; **22** *fly to Hamilton;* **23** three-day match v Northern Districts, Hamilton; **25** *travel by road to Auckland;* **26** Auckland-Sydney; **29-2 February** Bicentenary Test, Sydney; **3** *travel to Melbourne;* **4** one-day international v Australia, Melbourne; **6** *Melbourne-Auckland-New Plymouth;* **7-9** three-day match v Shell XI, New Plymouth; **10** *travel to Christchurch;* **12-17** First Test, Christchurch; **18** *to Dunedin;* **19-21** three-day match v President's XI Dunedin; **22** *travel to Auckland;* **25-29** Second Test, Auckland; **29** *travel to Wellington;* **3-7 March** Third Test, Wellington; **8** *travel to Dunedin;* **9** one-day international, Dunedin; **12** one-day international, Christchurch; **16** one-day international, Napier; **19** one-day international Auckland; **21** *Depart 11.30;* **22** *arrive Heathrow.*